The Faerie Queene

EDUCATING THE READER

Twayne's Masterwork Studies
Robert Lecker, General Editor

The Faerie Queene

EDUCATING THE READER

Russell J. Meyer

TWAYNE PUBLISHERS • BOSTON

A Division of G. K. Hall & Co.

Twayne's Masterwork Studies No. 73

Copyright 1991 by G. K. Hall & Co.
All rights reserved.
Published by Twayne Publishers
A division of G. K. Hall & Co.
70 Lincoln Street
Boston, Massachusetts 02111

Copyediting supervised by Barbara Sutton.
Book production by Gabrielle B. McDonald.
Typeset by World Composition Services Inc., Sterling, VA.

10 9 8 7 6 5 4 3 2 1 (hc)
10 9 8 7 6 5 4 3 2 1 (pb)

Library of Congress Cataloging-in-Publication Data

Meyer, Russell J.
    The Faerie queene : educating the reader / Russell J. Meyer.
        p.   cm. — (Twayne's masterwork studies ; no. 73)
    Includes bibliographical references and index.
    ISBN 0-8057-8076-9. — ISBN 0-8057-8122-6 (pbk.)
    1. Spenser, Edmund, 1552?–1599. Faerie queene. I. Title.
II. Series.
PR2358.M45   1991
821'.3—dc20   91-10182

Contents

Note on the References
and Acknowledgments

In attempting to provide a basic understanding of Spenser's great poem, I have assumed that the interested reader has completed (or is reading) the entire *Faerie Queene* and has ready access to a copy of the entire poem. Several complete versions of *The Faerie Queene* are available, although I have depended throughout on A. C. Hamilton's excellent edition (London: Longman, 1977). With its readable and accurate introductions and particularly helpful notes and commentary, Hamilton's edition of *The Faerie Queene* can only be called invaluable for any serious student of Spenser.

Students may, however, prefer to turn to the edition by Thomas P. Roche, Jr. (New Haven: Yale University Press, 1981); while the notes in this edition are equally excellent, they are not so copious, and it is certainly a more portable size. Finally, the *Variorum* edition of *The Works of Edmund Spenser* (Baltimore: Johns Hopkins University Press, 1932–49) is invaluable—although dated—for its extensive notes and summaries of early commentary. At 11 large volumes, however, it is very expensive and more likely to be found on a library shelf than in the private study of even the most devoted Spenserian.

Selections from *The Faerie Queene* are, of course, widely available in such collections as the Norton or Oxford anthologies of English literature. More comprehensive selections and critical commentary may be found in Hugh Maclean's Norton Critical Edition of *Edmund Spenser's Poetry*, 2d ed. (New York: W. W. Norton, 1982) or Robert Kellogg and Oliver Steele's edition, which includes Books I and II, the

Cantos of Mutabilitie, and selections from the minor poetry (New York: Odyssey, 1965).

For beginning students of Spenser, and even those familiar with his poem, I must offer a caveat. Interest in Spenser has greatly increased in the past dozen years, as even a glance at the contents of major literary journals or the papers presented at scholarly conferences will readily verify. There is both a newsletter, *Spenser Newsletter,* and an annual journal, *Spenser Studies,* devoted exclusively to Spenser, and our understanding of his intentions for *The Faerie Queene* grows almost daily. This book is not intended to bring you up to date in Spenser studies; rather it is intended to help you begin your studies with a basic understanding of the poem, which in turn will allow you to better appreciate and evaluate more detailed and advanced studies you may find elsewhere.

There are many people I would like to thank for their help and encouragement over the years, but perhaps the easiest way of doing that is simply to thank those who have made "Spenser at Kalamazoo" such a special event each year. Two people in particular, though, deserve special thanks by name for their part in this project. John Pendergast allowed me the benefit of his expertise in matters of Renaissance law, for which I am deeply grateful. Sarah Feeny read the entire manuscript and always managed to find something kind and helpful to say, no matter how muddled my thoughts and prose had become. Without her help this study would still be just an outline. Sheryl Mylan gave generously of her time for proofreading, a thankless task for which I can only offer my thanks. And finally, I would like to thank my students, who made me want to go to work each day, and Helga, Geoff, and Hillary, who made me want to come home.

Chronology:
Edmund Spenser's Life and Works

1485	Henry Tudor, the Earl of Richmond defeats and kills King Richard III at the Battle of Bosworth Field, succeeding him as King Henry VII and beginning the Tudor dynasty, which will continue until Queen Elizabeth's death in 1603, four years after Spenser's death.
1509	Henry VII dies; his son, Henry VIII, ascends the throne and marries Catherine of Aragon, the first of his six wives. Twelve years later, Henry will be awarded the title "Defender of the Faith" for his authorship of *Assertio septem sacramentorum,* a tract against Martin Luther's break with the Roman Catholic Church. The document may well have actually been written by Henry's friend and advisor Sir Thomas More.
1533	Elizabeth, daughter of Anne Boleyn, is born, the second child of Henry VIII.
1534	Henry VIII breaks with the Roman Catholic Church over the issue of divorce (and, presumably, political power in England). The following year, More is tried and executed for treason, a result of his refusal to agree to Henry's break.
1542	James V of Scotland dies and is succeeded by his six-day-old daughter, Mary, Queen of Scots, who will later figure in plots against her cousin Queen Elizabeth—and who will be portrayed by Spenser as Duessa.
1546	Martin Luther dies.
1547	Henry VIII dies; Edward VI, the son of Henry and Jane Seymour, takes the throne. Now only 10 years old, he will live to be 16.
1552	Edmund Spenser born, probably in London. Both the year and the birthplace are extrapolated from his poetry. *Amoretti* 60

places him at about 40 in 1592, while in *Prothalamion* he refers to London as "my most kyndly nurse / That to me gave this lifes first native sourse" (ll. 128–129).

1553	Edward VI dies and is succeeded by his Catholic half-sister, Mary, the daughter of Henry VIII and his first wife, Catherine of Aragon. Mary reestablishes ties with the Roman Catholic Church, an allegiance she strengthens by marrying the future Philip II of Spain.
1558	Queen Mary dies; Elizabeth I, the daughter of Henry VIII and Anne Boleyn, becomes Queen of England. Elizabeth turns England once more toward her father's Protestant religion, reaffirming that the English monarch is Supreme Head of the Church in England.
1559	Amidst arguments over Elizabeth's legitimacy, Mary, Queen of Scots takes for herself the title "Queen of England," after her husband, Francis II of France, succeeds his father to the throne.
1564	William Shakespeare and Galileo Galilei are both born. Michelangelo dies.
1561–1569	Spenser is a student at the Merchant Tailor's School in London, where he studies with Richard Mulcaster, who will later be known primarily for his tracts on education. While there, Spenser participates in poetic translations ("The Visions of Petrarch" and "The Visions of DuBellay"), which will appear in the *Theatre for Worldlings,* edited by Jan Van der Noot.
1570	At Pembroke College, Cambridge, Spenser makes friends with Gabriel Harvey; sometime during his tenure at Cambridge, he travels to the north country and meets "Rosalind"—if we are to take E.K.'s references in *The Shepheardes Calender* as accurately reflecting both the poem and Spenser's activities.
1573	Receives his B.A. in January.
1576	Receives his M.A. in June.
1577	Sir Francis Drake begins his voyage around the world. Spenser probably begins working on *The Shepheardes Calender.* Sometime during this year or the next two, he begins working on *The Faerie Queene,* a project that is to last the remainder of his life.
1578	Serves as secretary to Bishop Young of Rochester, whom he will represent as "Roffyn" in the September eclogue of *The Shepheardes Calender.*

Chronology

1579 *The Shepheardes Calender* published anonymously by Hugh Singleton in London.

1580 Sent to Ireland with Lord Grey, the Queen's Deputy in Ireland. Spenser's experiences there are reflected not only in his poetry (particularly Book V of *The Faerie Queene*), but also in his *Viewe of the present state of Ireland,* not published until 34 years after his death. In 1580 *Three proper, and wittie, familiar Letters* and *Two other, very commendable Letters* are also published, the correspondence between Spenser and his Cambridge friend, Gabriel Harvey. To what extent these letters were originally intended—or revised—for publication we cannot be certain, but they seem to have been intended for a broader readership than just the addressees.

1581 Appointed Registrar of the Faculties in the Court of Chancery, Dublin, a post he holds until June 1588.

1587 Spenser's friend and neighbor in Ireland, Sir Walter Ralegh, founds the first English colony in Virginia.

1588 The Spanish Armada is defeated and the Spanish threat to England greatly diminished. Abraham Fraunce quotes a stanza of *The Faerie Queene* (II.iv.35) in his *Arcadian Rhetoricke,* indicating that at least a segment of the poem was privately circulating at this time.

1590 Spenser is in London for the publication by William Ponsonby of Books I–III of *The Faerie Queene*. Spenser appends to the text an explanatory letter to Sir Walter Ralegh, dated 23 January 1589. Ralegh takes Spenser to court, where Spenser seeks preferment from the Queen. She grants him a £50 annual allotment. Spenser seems to consider the amount parsimonious, but it is still a significant sum in a time when a master craftsman might earn no more than £5 for a year's labor. By May of this year, Spenser is back in Ireland again.

1591 In December Spenser dedicates *Colin Clout's Come Home Again* to Ralegh, although the poem will not be published until four years later.

1594 Marries Elizabeth Boyle, daughter of an Anglo-Irish family, on 11 June, an event memorialized in *Epithalamion*. Their courtship, recorded in the *Amoretti,* began in 1592. This may well have been his second marriage, for a 1579 record indicates the marriage between "Edmonde Spenser" and a woman with the unlikely name of Maccabaeus Chylde, of whom nothing else is known.

1595   *Colin Clout's Come Home Again, Amoretti,* and *Epithalamion,* are published by William Ponsonby. The latter two are bound together in a single volume.

1596   Books IV–VI of *The Faerie Queene,* along with Books I–III, are published. Some revisions are made to the original ending of Book III. In this same year, *Fowre Hymns* and *Prothalamion* published, the latter reflecting Spenser's disappointment at not receiving further preferment as well as celebrating a betrothal.

1598   Driven from his Kilcolman home by the Irish rebels led by Tyrone, Spenser and his family return to London, where he appears in Elizabeth's court in December.

1599   Dies on 13 January and is buried in Westminster Abbey, near the grave of Chaucer, at the direction of Essex.

1603   Queen Elizabeth dies, ending the 118-year reign of the Tudor monarchs. Her choice of successors, James I of Scotland, the son of Mary, Queen of Scots, becomes James VI of England.

1609   *Two Cantos of Mutabilitie,* published by Matthew Lownes. Spenser's exact intentions for this fragment cannot be known, but it is nonetheless a fitting ending for *The Faerie Queene.*

1633   *A viewe of the present state of Ireland,* Spenser's only extended prose work, is published.

Literary and Historical Context

1

The English Renaissance

It is virtually impossible to understand *The Faerie Queene* without understanding something of the age that produced it: the English Renaissance. Every era may, perhaps, be characterized as "an era of change," but that appellation seems especially appropriate for the Renaissance, that vast period which stretches (in England at least) from the ascension of the first Tudor monarch, Henry VII, in 1485, through the restoration of the monarchy in 1660. This period saw momentous discoveries—the New World not being the least of those; the rise of new sciences and technologies, including the advent of movable print and the inexpensive books this technology permitted; a new cosmology, promulgated by the new astronomy that began to take seriously the notion of a heliocentric universe, one in which all the known world did not necessarily reflect God's grand plan for order and harmony; greatly revised forms of government leading to a renewed emphasis on education; and new (or at least significantly revised) forms of accepted religion. All of these factors are examined in greater detail elsewhere, but let us at least give three of them more than just a passing glance: the new monarchies, the Reformation, and the role of Tudor humanism.

THE RISE OF THE TUDORS

In 1485, Henry VII came to the throne, uniting the warring factions of Lancaster and York and establishing the Tudor dynasty, which was to last until the death of his granddaughter and Spenser's queen, Elizabeth I, in 1603. Henry brought with him to the throne not only peace, but also the English version of what has come to be known as the "New Monarchies." Much earlier, in the Middle Ages, centralized and powerful monarchies had existed throughout Europe, but they had given way to loose conglomerations of powerful and less powerful nobles who allowed the king to rule, either for the sake of convenience or for the sake of form. Now, however, powerful central monarchies were being renewed as the kings of Europe asserted their dominance over their nobles and the common people. Henry was the first English king to do just that, consolidating power in his own hands and turning the monarchy from symbol to reality.

But he also brought something entirely new to English rule: recognizing that government can best operate under the guidance of able bureaucrats, he stressed the importance of ability rather than mere birth as an instrument of advancement in the court and government. This policy played a large role in establishing the importance of education among the English, for if ability and not birth is a prime requisite for political success, if commoner and noble must compete equally for advancement, then education takes on an immensely more important role than it could ever have had in a society in which governing was limited to those of privileged birth.

THE REFORMATION

The change in the role of education had barely gotten underway when it was supplemented by vast changes in religion as well, changes that had far-reaching effects on both politics and education. In 1517, Martin Luther posted his 95 Theses on the doors of the cathedral in Wittenberg, effectively beginning his attempts to reform the established church. In 1521 Henry VIII, second of the Tudor kings, wrote a tract denouncing Luther and arguing for the supremacy of the Roman Church. Thirteen years later, having earned the honorific title "Defender of the Faith" for his literary efforts, Henry broke with Rome over his right to divorce Catherine of Aragon and marry the English Anne Boleyn, who, he hoped, would prove able to produce for him a son and heir. Religion, always an important issue in the Middle Ages, was now even more crucial for practical and nationalistic rather than just theological reasons.

By the time Spenser began work on *The Faerie Queene*, England had undergone vast changes in its religious orientation: from Catholic to Protestant under Henry VIII, violently back to Catholicism in the reign of his elder daughter, Mary, and then back once more just as violently to Protestantism under Elizabeth. It is little wonder religious and theological issues play such a large role in *The Faerie Queene* and other literature of the day.

HUMANISM

But religion was not the only subject of change. By the middle of the second decade of the sixteenth century, classical texts were widely available in Europe, thanks largely to the efforts of Aldius Mantuis, founder of the Aldine Press, which, beginning in 1511, had used the relatively new technology of movable print to issue inexpensive editions of virtually the entire corpus of classical literature as we know it today. And, thanks to the movement of learning from the East, there were scholars available in Europe who could teach Greek, so the new texts were not wasted on ignorant readers. By the time Henry VIII died in 1547, the classics were the mainstay of English education. St. Paul's School had been founded in 1509, and it was soon followed by many institutions devoted to the new education. By the time Elizabeth came to the throne in 1558, such educators as Roger Ascham and Spenser's schoolmaster, Richard Mulcaster, had established the new education as the norm.

Education flourished in the sixteenth century for three reasons: the availability of books; the need for educated courtiers in the government of the Tudors; and the new interests in the classics and in scholarship, thanks to those whom we have since called the "humanists."

A popular misconception about the Renaissance is that these humanists, placing their interests in humanity and an anthropocentric universe, abandoned religion, preferring the secular life. Nothing, in fact, could be less correct. True, the humanists were more likely to concern themselves with things of this world, to perceive the world in less theological terms than their medieval ancestors. They were more likely to concentrate on the present life on earth rather than on the afterlife in Paradise, and they were likely to hold Greek and Roman— pagan—authors in far higher regard than their medieval forebears. But they were nonetheless profoundly religious, and their religion pervaded their everyday life. One need look no further than Book I of *The Faerie Queene,* "The Legend of Holinesse," with its familiar allusions to religious and theological concerns, to see the extent to which religion was held dear by the humanists and their students.

But the knights Spenser uses as his examples "to fashion a gentleman or noble person"[1] are politically and socially involved, not merely contemplative. Their role is in the world of action, not the world of prayer, although prayer always forms an important part of their lives. In the newly rediscovered classical literature the Renaissance humanists found precisely the examples for behavior that best suited their needs. The educated man (and it was virtually always men who received formal education) was trained to play important roles in governing the nation, an ideal expressed in such classical authors as Cicero and Quintilian. This classical concept did not fit well with the medieval ideal of the contemplative life, but, in this new era, it added the respectability of tradition to the necessity of practice. In the Ciceronian ideal the humanists saw exactly what England needed: orators who were concerned intensely with the good of the nation. Literary and political life, they saw, could be as successfully melded as religious and political life, and hence so could literature, politics, and education. Spenser's desire then for "vertuous and gentle discipline" is typical not only of his age, but of Cicero and Quintilian as well. The "new" classics had formed the new orthodoxy. Aristotle may have concentrated in his *Rhetoric* on the importance of learning and oratory, but Cicero and Quintilian furnished for the Renaissance the importance of the character of the orator—and hence the importance of moral instruction as an integral part of preparation for the active life.

Life and learning became inseparably united, and as humanist scholarship developed and study of the classics became more and more an integral part of Renaissance education, the world of classical authors became as much a part of reality for the well-educated man as his daily living experiences.

It is, then, in this context of change and discovery that Spenser produced his masterwork. And perhaps it should not be surprising that it looks so clearly toward the past, for in an era of such unsettling changes, the past looks more solid, comforting, dependable than it otherwise might. In dwelling on knights' and ladies' gentle deeds, Spenser is reflecting the same conservatism that led his queen to revise the rules of armed combat, rules that had been untouched for nearly 100 years[2]; tournaments, armed combats featuring knights and armor long made obsolete by new weaponry and new modes of war, once again graced England. The past, it seems, looked comfortable to those in the midst of change.

If there is any single characteristic that stands out in the English Renaissance, perhaps it is this striving toward the future while looking longingly to the past. That, in fact, may be why the literature of the period still holds such a grip on readers today, for we join them in celebrating our future and longing for our past. And perhaps no writer of the entire English Renaissance better represents that dual vision than Edmund Spenser, and no work better than *The Faerie Queene*.

2

The Importance of *The Faerie Queene*

Defending poetry against its detractors in the early 1580s, Spenser's great contemporary Sir Philip Sidney compares the poet to the astronomer, the mathematician, the musician, the philosopher, the lawyer, even the historian, and finds all the others wanting:

> Nature never set forth the earth in so rich tapistry as divers poets have done, neither with so pleasant rivers, fruitful trees, sweet-smelling flowers, not whatsoever else may make the too much loved earth more lovely. Her world is brasen, the poets only deliver a golden. But let those things alone and go to man (for whom as the other things are, so it seemeth in him her uttermost cunning is employed), and know whether she have brought forth so true a lover as Theagines, so constant a friend as Pylades, so valiant a man as Orlando, so right a Prince as Xenophon's Cyrus, and so excellent a man in every way, as Virgil's Aeneas. Neither let this be jestingly conceived because the works of the one be essential, the other in imitation of fiction, for every understanding knoweth the skill of each artificer standeth in that Idea or foreconceit of the work, and not in the work itself. And that the poet hath that Idea, is manifest, by delivering them forth in such excellency as he had imagined them.

> Which delivering forth also is not wholly imaginative, as we are
> wont to say by them that build castles in air, but so far substantially
> it worketh, not onely to make a Cyrus, which had been but a
> particular excellency, as Nature might have done, but to bestow a
> Cyrus upon the world to make many Cyruses, if they will learn
> aright why and how that maker made him.[3]

Sidney did not have the advantage of seeing *The Faerie Queene* before
his untimely death in 1586, but if he had he surely would have used
Spenser's masterwork to demonstrate the truth of his proposition that
poets create a "golden" world, for in *The Faerie Queene*, we find
exactly that.

Spenser not only creates a world in his Faerie Land and peoples it
with characters who engage our imagination, but also mirrors our own
world and shows us ourselves. Those characteristics can be seen in the
way that *The Faerie Queene*, 400 years after the publication of its first
three books, still holds the attention of readers, even those unfamiliar
with, even uninterested in, the historical events that inform so much
of the poem. The value of *The Faerie Queene* rests not just in the
beauties and intricacies of Spenser's poetry, not just in the historical
allegory, or even its superb moral coloration. Rather, as I hope I will
demonstrate in the following pages, its value rests on Spenser's ability
to draw us into his work, not just to appreciate and understand it, but
to learn from it and to grow to a better understanding of the human
condition.

In the denizens of Faerie Land we see not just knights and ladies
who must face their own deepest fears, but ourselves, just as clearly as
Spenser's contemporaries must have seen themselves in Redcrosse,
Una, Guyon, Britomart, or Calidore. We need not identify directly
with Guyon's knightly accoutrements or the Redcrosse Knight's deep
religious devotion to see in them our own need to achieve temperance
or behave faithfully to our God or to our companions. Here, then, is
the true value of *The Faerie Queene*: it speaks directly to our deepest
convictions and helps us better understand not just what it means to
be human, but what it means to exist in society.

By following the adventures of the Redcrosse Knight we learn not just the value of orthodox sixteenth-century theology, but the nature of devotion of all kinds and what it means to our very existence. From Sir Guyon we learn the value of temperance, and from the adventures of Britomart and Artegall we learn more of our relationships with others. Finally, from Calidore and the other characters of Book VI we learn not just courteous behavior, but what it means to have a duty and how important it is that we remain faithful to that duty and to ourselves.

Spenser says that with his poem he hopes to "fashion a gentleman or noble person in vertuous and gentle discipline." Little could he know that 400 years later, he would still be achieving that end with readers of *The Faerie Queene*.

3

The Critical Reception

"What mankind have long possessed they have often examined and compared; and if they persist to value the possession, it is because frequent comparisons have confirmed opinion in its favour."[4] This is Samuel Johnson's rationale for veneration of "ancient" literature (and by "ancient," in this particular essay, he means Shakespeare, who died only about a century earlier). There are those, of course, who would argue such a view. Mere age and earlier fame can hardly be the sole determiner of our present attitudes toward a work of art. Indeed, literary fortunes rise and fall as regularly and precipitously as the stock market, and we would (as Dr. Johnson also reminds us) be mistaken to venerate a work of literature merely because it is old or even merely because earlier generations of readers have valued it. If it has no value for readers in our own age, then our interest in it can be only antiquarian.

But this is most certainly not the case with *The Faerie Queene,* for it has not only pleased many and pleased long, but continues today to speak to readers who come to the poem for the first or the fifth time.

One could, of course, argue that the first critical work on *The*

Faerie Queene is Spenser's own letter to Sir Walter Ralegh, appended
to the 1590 edition of Books I–III of the poem, if by "criticism" we
mean simply commentary upon a work. Using such a definition we
would certainly also include the seven "Commendatory Verses" that
first appeared with *The Faerie Queene*. But these are songs of praise,
not analytic examinations of the poem. And in his letter Spenser makes
clear that his goal is less to illuminate the poem than to prepare the
reader, "to direct your vnderstanding to the wel-head of the History,
that from thence gathering the whole intention of the conceit, ye may
as in a handfull gripe al the discourse, which otherwise may happily
seeme tedious and confused." Most of what we might call "critical
statements" prior to the eighteenth century, in fact, are more along the
line of appreciative remarks. Not that these should be ignored, of
course, for they certainly reflect the attitudes of Spenser's early readers
toward his poem. And when John Milton calls Spenser "a better teacher
than *Scotus* or *Aquinas*" in his *Areopagitica,* he does more than just
state an appreciation: he sets the tenor of much Spenser criticism to
follow.

   Most of the early appreciative remarks have at their heart a recognition of Spenser's demonstration that English is fit to be a poetic
language, as Joseph Hall comments in his *Virgidamiarum*:

> Salust of *France* and *Tuscan Ariost,*
> Yield vp the *Lawrell girlond* ye haue lost:
> And let all others willow weare with mee,
> Or let their vnd[e]seuring *Temples* bared be.[5]

   Later commentary turned from appreciations to more thorough
analytic examinations of *The Faerie Queene,* although at times the
criticism reflects the critic and his age more than it illuminates Spenser's
poem. Among such writers is John Dryden who, while he praises
Spenser for having both "genius" and "Learning," nonetheless finds
that there is "no Uniformity in the Design of Spencer: He aims at the
Accomplishment of no one Action: He raises up a Hero for every one

of his Adventures; and endows each of them with some particular Moral Virtue, which rends them all equal, without Subordination or Preference."[6] Dryden is, however, generous when compared to Joseph Addison, who seems to find nothing worthy of praise in Spenser:

> Old Spencer next, warm'd with Poetic Rage,
> In Antick Tales amus'd a Barb'rous Age;
> An Age that yet uncultivate and Rude,
> Where-e're the Poet's Fancy led, pursu'd
> Through pathless Fields, and unfrequented Floods,
> To Dens of Dragons, and Enchanted Woods.
> But now that Mystick Tale, that pleas'd of Yore
> Can Charm an understanding Age no more;
> The long-spun Allegories fulsom grow,
> While the dull Moral lyes too plain below.[7]

We should not dismiss eighteenth-century criticism on the basis of Addison's remarks, tempting though it may be, for Pope demonstrates a fine understanding of Spenser (as least as a pastoral poet), and the same century produced both John Upton's annotations for his edition of *The Faerie Queene* and John Hughes's preface to his collection of Spenser's *Works*.

The most famous nineteenth-century view of *The Faerie Queene* is surely that of William Hazlitt, who reminds readers that they need not be frightened away by the allegory: "But some people will say that . . . they cannot understand it on account of the allegory. They are afraid of the allegory, as if they thought it would bite them: they look at it as a child looks at a painted dragon, and think it will strangle them in its shining folds. This is very idle. If they do not meddle with the allegory, the allegory will not meddle with them."[8]

Writing at about the same time, Samuel Taylor Coleridge finds (not surprisingly) the effects of the fancy and imagination in *The Faerie Queene*:

> Lastly, the great and prevailing character of Spenser's mind is fancy under the conditions of imagination, as an ever present but not

always active power. He has an imaginative fancy, but he has not imagination, in kind or degree, as Shakespeare and Milton have; the boldest effort of his powers in this way is the character of Talus. Add to this a feminine tenderness and almost maidenly purity of feeling, and above all, a deep moral earnestness which produces a believing sympathy and acquiescence in the reader, and you have a tolerably adequate view of Spenser's intellectual being.[9]

Coleridge certainly appreciated Spenser, although he just as certainly seems to have misapprehended both the intent and the content of *The Faerie Queene* and thus misleads in stating that Talus represents Spenser's "boldest effort." And in asserting that Spenser is possessed of a "maidenly purity of feeling" and "deep moral earnestness" he reinforces the timorous approach to *The Faerie Queene* Hazlitt is trying to help his readers avoid.

Hazlitt's advice is, in fact, worth attending to, for those who conceive of *The Faerie Queene* as a "scholar's poem" let the allegory frighten them away from the experience of it. To view the poem as a mere collection of obscure references is to rob it of many, if not all, of its excellencies and to deprive oneself of its poetry. But excessive attention to the poetry at the expense of the allegory is just as danger-ous, and that is where Hazlitt's remarks were to lead later in the nineteenth century among readers who turned away entirely from the depths of *The Faerie Queene* to attend only to its surface.

That prevailing view was challenged in the early twentieth century by scholars who sought to uncover the mysteries beneath the poem's surface, to turn once more to its allegory. But a mere return to such matters does not necessarily entail a more profitable view of the whole of the poem. Nevertheless, of primary importance in the early twentieth century was the work of Spenser's academic critics, perhaps better called "scholars," to turn to an old-fashioned but still valuable distinc-tion between "criticism" and "scholarship." Their bibliographic and textual work may be said to culminate in the Johns Hopkins University Press edition of *The Works of Edmund Spenser,* known popularly as the "*Variorum* Spenser," a massive 11-volume compendium of earlier (and contemporary) scholarship and critical views, under the general editorship of Edwin Greenlaw, Charles Grosvenor Osgood, F. M. Padelford, and Ray Heffner.

While the critical views represented in the *Variorum* edition may be dated, it is still the first place to turn to identify a historical personage or pin down an obscure allusion. The *Variorum* is certainly a monument to Spenser scholarship. At the same time, however, the very monumentality of the work may have reinforced the fears Hazlitt warned against, for in the first half of the twentieth century, *The Faerie Queene* was seen largely as outside the domain of anyone not specially trained to read it. If for earlier periods, Spenser had been seen as a "poet's poet," for the early twentieth century he was faced with the even more condemnatory view of being a "scholar's poet."

Criticism in the second half of the twentieth century, however, has rescued Spenser from these titles—or perhaps shown that both are correct yet each is in itself incomplete. An earlier generation of critics, including such luminaries as C. S. Lewis (particularly in *The Allegory of Love*) and Rosemond Tuve (especially in her *Allegorical Imagery*), provided the basis for the growth of Spenser criticism since about 1960. With the diminishing influence of the "New Criticism," Spenser was once more recognized as a poet who could offer insights to more than just other poets or deeply committed scholars of Renaissance poetry. The value of *The Faerie Queene* is no longer the subject of debate.

As the twentieth century moved into its final decades, the league of Spenserians increased to include those whose critical views would have amazed if not mystified the *Variorum* editors or the "appreciators" of still earlier times. I have open before me as I write the Fall 1988 issue of *Spenser Newsletter* with the "Spenser Bibliography Update" for 1986. There I find listed some 125 works—books, chapters, articles—devoted in whole or in part to Spenser, over half of which are concerned primarily with *The Faerie Queene*. These cover the full range of contemporary critical and scholarly endeavors, ranging from new studies in Spenser's sources and influences to feminist psychoanalytic analyses of characters and episodes. Some require specialized scholarly knowledge of Spenser and his age; others come closer to the category of "appreciations." But all share a concern with the poet and his poem, and all Spenserians would agree that the way to start a study of *The Faerie Queene* is with the poem itself.

A Reading

4

An Introduction

In the "October" eclogue of *The Shepheardes Calender*, Spenser's first major published work, one of the speakers, a shepherd named Piers, attempts to persuade a poet-shepherd, Cuddie, that he should turn his attention from lesser forms of poetry to the epic:

> Abandon then the base and viler clowne,
> Lyft up they selfe out of the lowly dust:
> And sing of bloody Mars, of wars, of giusts.
> Turne thee to those that weld the awful crowne,
> To doubted Knights, whose woundlesse armour rusts,
> And helmes unbruzed wexen dayly browne.
>
> There may thy Muse display her fluttryng wing,
> And stretch her selfe at large from East to West:
> Wither thou list in fayre *Elisa* rest,
> Or if thee please in bigger notes to sing,
> Advaunce the worthy whome shee loveth best,
> That first the white beare to the stake did bring.[10]

Cuddie, however, is a less than fully insightful poet, for he argues that all the good topics for epic poetry are already taken, and he disregards

Piers's advice to sing of Elizabeth ("fayre Elisa") or even her courtly favorite (and Spenser's patron) Leicester ("the worthy whom shee loveth best"). There is, though, Cuddie says, another poet capable of such flights: Colin, the very figure of a poet in *The Shepheardes Calender,* the character we are apparently meant to take as Spenser himself.

Cuddie may not be willing to turn from more rustic to more elegant poetry, but Colin seems to have abandoned poetry altogether. In the "January" eclogue, the beginning of the poem, he has broken his shepherd's pipe, a traditional symbol for the poet's instrument, and in his final farewell in "December," he appears to be leaving forever:

> Gather ye together my little flocke,
> My little flock, that was to me so liefe:
> Let me, ah lette me in your folds ye lock,
> Ere the breme Winter breede you greater griefe.
>> Winter is come, that blowes the balefull breath,
>> And after winter commeth timely death.
>
> Adieu delightes, that lulled me asleepe,
> Adieu my deare, whose love I bought so deare:
> Adieu my little Lambes and loved sheepe,
> Adieu ye Woodes that oft my witnesse were:
>> Adieu good *Hobbinol,* that was so true;
>> Tell *Rosalind,* her *Colin* bids her adieu.
>
> (ll. 145–156)

Colin has said his adieus, but he is not gone, for he makes another appearance in *The Faerie Queene,* Book VI, where Sir Calidore finds him singing a beautiful song. More important, Colin's voice at the end of *The Shepheardes Calender* seems to be the very same voice that opens *The Faerie Queene,* the voice of a poet who recognizes that he has served his poetic apprenticeship and is now ready to embark on a more challenging task:

> Lo! I the man, whose Muse whilome did maske,
>> As time her taught, in lowly Shepheards weeds,
> Am now enforst a farre vnfitter taske,

An Introduction

For trumpets sterne to chaunge mine Oaten reeds,
And sing of Knights and Ladies gentle deeds;
Whose prayses hauing slept in silence long,
Me, all too meane, the sacred Muse areeds
To blazon broade emongst her learned throng:
Fierce warres and faithfull loues shall moralize my song.

(I.Proem.i)

This is not a new poet; this is a new song, a new task for which the poet has prepared himself, like Vergil before and Milton after, by concentrating first on lesser forms, by perfecting his craft in those forms, then turning to that highest poetic endeavor, the epic. And it is not coincidental that in identifying himself (or his speaker) as the poet who once wore "lowly Shepheards weeds" and used "Oaten reeds," Spenser tacitly acknowledges authorship of *The Shepheardes Calender*. If there were any literate members of Elizabethan society who did not know the progenitor of that pastoral poem, this first stanza of the new poem would leave them fully informed. Only a poet fully conscious of himself in a poetic role could so clearly announce his intentions and his fitness for the task at hand.

How well Spenser had prepared himself for this task can perhaps be seen by looking not at *The Faerie Queene*, but at *The Shepheardes Calender*, the poem upon which Spenser's contemporary reputation was already made. It is possible to read and fully understand *The Faerie Queene* without ever turning to the earlier work, but it is not possible to fully understand Spenser's impact upon English poetry without first paying some attention to *The Shepheardes Calender*, for it is surely the most important poetic production since Chaucer's *Canterbury Tales*. It is a poetic experiment that may well rank with those of Wordsworth and Coleridge's *Lyrical Ballads* or T. S. Eliot's *Prufrock and Other Poems*: it marks the beginning of a new poetic era and is unlike anything that precedes it.

The Shepheardes Calender consists of twelve sections, called *eclogues*, one for each month of the year, ranging from 78 lines ("January") to 317 lines ("May"). Its characters are shepherds and their companions, but their concerns are far from rustic. In addition to poetic concerns, the poem contains allegorical references to contemporary political and religious events—a fit preparation for the poet whose major work would contain layer after layer of allegory. Eleven characters appear in the various eclogues, and many others—including some only thinly disguised representations of Spenser's contemporaries—are directly mentioned or alluded to. There are, in all, 13 different verse forms, ranging from simple tetrameter couplets to a delightfully complex sestina. One, the eight-line stanza of "November," approximates the *Faerie Queene* stanza, but without the final Alexandrine.

There are, of course, many issues to consider with regard to *The Shepheardes Calender,* not the least of which is C. S. Lewis's charge that "it commits the one sin for which, in literature, no merits can compensate; it is rather dull."[11] For our purposes, however, it is sufficient to point out the impact *The Shepheardes Calender* had upon the reading public. To say that it was a sensation may well be to mistake contemporary commentary upon it with the blinders provided by hindsight. But it was surely recognized as an important and significant work, and its anonymous poet was singled out for praise by Sir Philip Sidney and others. Sidney, in fact, finds little to praise in English poetry, limiting himself to Chaucer, the *Mirror for Magistrates,* Surrey's lyrics, and the anonymous author of *The Shepheardes Calender*: "*The Shepherds Calender* hath much poetry in his Eclogues, indeed worthy the reading, if I be not deceived. That same framing of his style to an old rustic language I dare not allow, since neither Theocritus in Greek, Virgil in Latin, nor Sannazaro in Italian did affect it."[12] That "old rustic language" is, of course, Spenser's homage to Chaucer, but it is also an attempt to return to that simpler time, a time when life and language and poetry were pure and golden.

William Webbe, in "A Discourse of English Poetrie" (1586), praises Spenser by name as "Master *Sp*: Author of the *Sheepeheardes Calender,* whose trauell in that peece of English Poetrie I thinke verely is so commendable, as none of equall iudgment can yeelde him lesse prayse for hys excellent skyll and skylfull excellency shwered forth in the same then they would to eyther *Theocritus* or *Virgill.*"[13] Thomas Nashe would "preferre diuine Master Spencer, the miracle of wit, to bandie line by line for my life, in the honour of England, against Spaine, France, Italy, and all the world" in any sort of battle of art and "deepe conceit."[14]

The Shepheardes Calender provided the proof of something the English had reason to doubt: that their language was indeed fit for verse. Chaucer was the last great poet to write in English, but the language had changed so much since his day that only a few could read him with full comprehension, and virtually none could scan his poetry, with its long forgotten stresses and pronunciations. The period between Chaucer's death in 1400 and 1579 had been largely fallow in terms of poetic production. The fifteenth century is practically barren, and the early sixteenth offers little better. There was, of course, John Skelton, but his poetry surely seemed to contemporary ears little more than doggerel (he is "called Poet Laureat for what reason I know not" Puttenham says of him in his *Arte of English Poetry*). Sir Thomas Wyatt and Henry Howard, Earl of Surrey, produced lovely verse—but they were largely translations from Italian originals. What English lacked, or so Spenser's contemporaries thought, was the power of Italian or French or Spanish, the variety necessary for true poetic production. With *The Shepheardes Calender* Spenser put such doubts to rest. Even if the language was archaic, the subject matter at times obscure, and the accompanying textual notes at best misleading, there were still all those different rhyme schemes and stanzaic forms, proof that English was suited to be a poetic language.

That proven, all that remained was to show that English was fit, too, for that most exalted of verse forms, the epic. And that brings us to *The Faerie Queene,* Spenser's homage to his poetic forebears, his religion, his nation, and his Queen.

Strictly speaking, *The Faerie Queene* is not an epic. After all, it does not reach the requisite 12 books, nor is it, like the *Iliad* or the *Odyssey,* an account of the exploits of a single hero, unless we pervert its narrative to claim such a primary role for Prince Arthur. Nonetheless, it does have what film publicists like to call "epic sweep," and it certainly concerns itself with the origins and worth of the English nation as well as Faerie Land. It is closer, though, to a form popular in contemporary Italy, the epic-romance (or romance-epic). It is influenced not only by classical models, but also by two great Italian poems of the sixteenth century, Torquato Tasso's *Gerusalemme Liberata* and Lodovico Ariosto's *Orlando Furioso*. The influence of these two works is so pervasive, in fact, that even to list specific episodes and shorter passages for which Spenser was indebted to Tasso and Ariosto would take several pages. But a mere list of passages would still not do justice to the influence particularly of Ariosto on Spenser's plans and methods for *The Faerie Queene*. The difficulties many readers have perceived with the episodic, disjointed nature of Books III and IV, for example, become far less problematic when the Ariostan methods are taken into account.[15] In general, an understanding of Italian Renaissance literature is central to a fuller appreciation of not just *The Faerie Queene,* but other sixteenth-century English literature as well.

THE FAERIE QUEENE AS PHYSICAL ARTIFACT

In his letter to Ralegh, appended to the 1590 publication of Books I–III of *The Faerie Queene,* Spenser projects 12 books for his poem, beginning with the adventures of the Redcrosse Knight and culminating with the opening events in Gloriana's court. Only 6 of the projected 12 books were completed, along with (at least) a fragment of a seventh (*The Cantos of Mutabilitie*). Each book has a proem of 5 to 11 stanzas, which sets the tone or the context of the book, plus 12 full cantos ranging in length from 30 to 87 stanzas each. There are, in all, some 3,837 nine-line stanzas—34,533 lines (or about 180,000 words). Each stanza rhymes *a b a b b c b c c;* the first eight lines are iambic pentameter, the ninth an Alexandrine (that is, iambic hexameter). That final line, with its extra syllables, has the effect not just of rounding out the stanza, but also of moving the reader forward to the next stanza, providing, as it were, a sort of impulse to continue with the reading, much as it must have provided for Spenser the impulse to continue with the writing.[16]

THE LETTER TO RALEGH

Dated 1589 and appearing with the first published version of *The Faerie Queene,* Spenser's letter to his friend Sir Walter Ralegh may reflect his early thoughts on the poem. The letter is dated 23 January 1589 but may in fact have been written earlier, perhaps originally, in fact, even to some other recipient. There are inconsistencies in the letter, deviations from the poem it purports to describe, that make the 1589 date suspect. But there are also comments that promote a better understanding of Spenser's view of his own poem. In particular, as he expresses it in the letter, Spenser sees a specific educational purpose for *The Faerie Queene:* "to fashion a gentleman or noble person in vertuous and gentle discipline." That purpose colors not only the events Spenser presents to us in the poem, but his method of presentation as well, for he continually seems to be attempting to ensure that his reader will indeed be "fashioned"—that is, educated—in the virtues he presents in his heroes.

We should also note in the letter Spenser's specific praises of Queen Elizabeth, for portraying her and her nation never seems to have been far from his mind. Furthermore, his remarks about Gloriana and Prince Arthur help us better understand their allegorical significances. In Gloriana, he says, "I meane glory in my generall intention, but in my particular I conceiue the most excellent and glorious person of our soueraine the Queene, and her kingdome in Faery land." And with Arthur he means to "sette forth magnificence."

Such remarks also help make clear that Spenser intended his poem to be read allegorically: there are, he says, those who would prefer their lessons in a more straightforward manner, but he has preferred to present them "thus clowdily enwrapped in Allegoricall deuices."

Although the letter can help us better understand Spenser's general intentions for *The Faerie Queene,* we must also be careful not to take it too literally, for while it is an accurate rendition of early events in Book I, it inaccurately reflects what happens in Book II, for example, indicating that the Palmer brings Ruddymane, the bloody handed-babe, to court: "The second day, ther came in a Palmer bearing an Infant with bloody hands, whose Parents he complained to haue bene slayn by an Enchaunteresse called Acrasia: and therfore craued of the Faery Queene, to appoint him some knight, to performe that aduenture, which being assigned to Sir Guyon, he presently went forth with that same Palmer: which is the beginning of the second booke and the whole subject thereof." In fact, Guyon and the Palmer happen upon the babe as they are traveling together, and it is at this point that Guyon swears to seek revenge on Acrasia.

Given such errors, we clearly cannot take the letter as gospel, but it nonetheless provides powerful clues about Spenser's intentions and methods that are necessary to understand and appreciate *The Faerie Queene.*

READING THE ALLEGORY OF *THE FAERIE QUEENE*

Most modern readers find the general surface of *The Faerie Queene* relatively difficult to follow. After all, the language is archaic, even by Elizabethan standards, and the values and events Spenser portrays are not always the most compatible with our own experiences. Even those who overcome the linguistic and intellectual barriers often find themselves faced with a still more difficult impasse: the allegory.

Spenser makes clear in his letter to Ralegh that he considers his poem "a continued Allegory, or darke conceit." Allegory should be relatively easy to define. We might say that allegory occurs "when the events of a narrative obviously and continuously refer to another simultaneous structure of events or ideas, whether historical events, moral or philosophical ideas, or natural phenomena."[17] One need not read very far into *The Faerie Queene*, however, to realize that such a definition is inadequate for this poem, for at times the allegory is neither obvious nor continuous, although we have no doubt that it is there. Let us, though, for the moment, be content that there are correspondences between the narrative of *The Faerie Queene* and "historical events, moral or philosophical ideas, or natural phenomena" of concern to Spenser and his contemporary readers.[18] It is in the relationship of the narrative to these events, ideas, and phenomena that we will find the allegory, if like Spenser's contemporaries, we can read the poem allegorically.

It is hard for us to imagine, as late twentieth-century readers, just how familiar the process of allegorizing would have been to Spenser and his contemporaries, for to us allegory is a literary rather than a living issue. We come to such poems as *The Faerie Queene* or even something as familiar as Orwell's *Animal Farm* unready to deal with multiple levels of meaning. Allegory simply is not part of our day-to-day lives.

For Spenser's upper-class readers, however, allegory was a far more familiar way of dealing with life. This may perhaps be best illustrated with a bit of evidence from Queen Elizabeth's court. As part of the entertainments of envoys sent from France to attempt an arrangement of marriage between the Queen and the Duke de Alençon, an elaborate tournament was held:

> The jousting was an allegory of seduction, in which the chaste Fortress of Beauty, representing the Queen herself, was besieged by Desire, or the ardent wooer Alençon. The Fortress was assaulted with mock cannons shooting perfumed water and "sweet powder," and the attackers threw flowers against the walls. But no assault on the queen's purity, however metaphorical, could be allowed to succeed. Desire's siege was turned back, and he was instructed by one of the actors in the pageantry to "content himself with a favorable parley, and wait for grace by loyalty."[19]

This was not an isolated event. Years earlier, in 1575, the Queen had been involved in a similar occurrence on the last day of her stay at the Earl of Leicester's home, Kenilworth:

> When the time came for Elizabeth to leave her departure drew sighs and doleful poems from a new set of allegorical figures. On her last day of hunting Sylvanus, god of the woods, appeared and urged her "forever to abide in this country," running along beside her horse and promising to double the number of deer in the chase and to make a continual spring in the gardens if only she would consent never to leave. Deepdesire, a messenger from the "council-chamber of heaven," addressed her in verse and, while a consort of musicians played in the background, sang his sad madrigal.[20]

Granted, both of these events involved the Queen, and thus there is reason to suspect that at other layers of society things would not have been the same. But the mere fact that such events occurred indicates a different way of viewing allegory and life, a way essentially alien to twentieth-century readers.

Knowing that the Elizabethans were capable of participating in allegory in their daily lives, however, does little for our ability to understand, indeed participate in, an allegorical poem. If we were so inclined, we could simply follow William Hazlitt's caveat in dealing with the poem: not worry about its allegory, but allow ourselves merely to be taken in with its luxurious surface. To do so may have served Hazlitt's purposes in an era where idolatry of Spenser seemed perhaps to threaten the very existence of contemporary poetry. It will not, however, serve our purposes today, when we seek a broader and deeper understanding of Spenser's aims and techniques.

We must, then, come face to face with the allegory, no matter how daunting the prospect. But how are we to read the allegory, to confront the difficulty not just of reading on a literal level a poem that is often frustratingly complex, but also of simultaneously recognizing that the poem has several layers or shades of meaning, some of which are not necessarily compatible with others?

An Introduction

In many ways, reading *The Faerie Queene* is unlike reading any other work of art, for it demands more than just a willing suspension of disbelief, but also a recognition that normal interpretations of texts do not necessarily hold here. We must be willing to recognize and appreciate not only the literal level of the story, the narrative, as it were, but also that each character, each action, has a meaning beyond the literal. In addition, there may be more than one such meaning and the meanings may shift, Proteus-like. A lion may represent Henry VIII, the Defender of the Faith, in one canto, and something horrid in another. It looks like the same lion, sounds like the same lion—but has become a very different allegorical figure.

The tendency among some modern readers is to dismiss such inconsistencies or to criticize Spenser for being something his contemporaries never would have expected him to be: consistent within the entire work, or at least within its individual books. If we are to read this poem well, however, we must dismiss our own demands for allegorical and narrative consistency, settling instead for the rich textures Spenser achieves through his infinite variety. We must be willing to set aside our preconceptions of how narratives, even allegories, should work, and we must be willing to allow the shifts Spenser demands; without such an attitude, we cannot successfully read *The Faerie Queene*.

Perhaps the easiest way of considering the allegory and narrative in *The Faerie Queene* is to follow A. C. Hamilton's advice in his edition of the poem and think of it as analogous to a dream. In a dream, events are connected in only the most tenuous ways, yet the dreamer doesn't question those connections. The same can be said for the poem; if we look for logical connections among its parts, we may be both confused and disconcerted. If, on the other hand, we are willing to accept that at one moment a lion may represent Henry VIII and all that is good in British history and at another the Roman Catholic Church and all that a loyal Renaissance Englishman might see as horrid, then we can get along with the poem. If we demand consistency of the surface narrative, then we are almost bound to be disappointed, just as we would be disappointed by our dreams if we really demanded such consistency of them.

There is a kind of consistency throughout the narrative of *The Faerie Queene,* but it is not the same kind of consistency we would expect from a nineteenth-century novel: Spenser is not writing a Renaissance *David Copperfield,* and to expect the same sorts of narrative techniques from him that we find in a nineteenth-century novelist would almost surely lead us to disappointment if not disgust. The trick, in short, to reading *The Faerie Queene* is to meet the poem on its own terms, to allow it its multiplicity of meanings and allow ourselves the freedom of interpretation that Spenser demands. Approaching the poem with a complex of preconceptions can result in our being misled into expecting something quite different from what is there.

THE MULTIPLE NARRATORS

Reading *The Faerie Queene* also requires that one be aware of multiple narrative voices throughout the poem. There is not, as in most other works of literature, a single narrator who is "reliable" or "unreliable," "omniscient" or "objective." At times the narrator who serves as our guide in *The Faerie Queene* is wholly objective, at times fully omniscient, at times naive. In fact, there are many portions of the poem where one senses more than a single narrator at work, as if there is a second voice, one we might call "the poet" (or even "Spenser") rather than just the "narrator." This is the voice that tells us that the "haven is nigh at hand" or that he intends to "delay until another canto" finishing an event or that he is "exhausted." This narrator serves as our guide, in effect, not presenting the chronology of events, but rather guiding our responses to what goes on in the poem. Spenser often uses this second (or "secondary") narrator to color our responses by giving us some generalizations at the opening of a canto that will determine how we are to react as that canto progresses. At the same time, however, he never stops playing games with us, giving us one reaction when in fact he wants us to have quite another. At the opening of the canto dealing with Timias and Belphoebe in Book III, for example, he discusses how various types of people are affected by love, spending a few lines on the responses of those of the "baser sort." Timias, hardly the baser sort, responds just as the baser people do—and thus reminds us that, regardless of social position and training, we all have the potential to be base.[21]

READING AND EXPERIENCE

Perhaps the most interesting experience in reading *The Faerie Queene*, however, has to do neither with the allegory per se nor with the multiple narrators, but rather with the constant challenges Spenser presents, essentially daring us to fall prey to the sins his various heroes are trying to overcome—and if we are not careful, we will indeed join the heroes in falling prey to those sins. If, for example, we believe that the Redcrosse Knight has actually overcome error by defeating the dragonlike monster Error and her offspring in canto i of Book I, then we are likely to fail to recognize that Redcrosse almost immediately falls into another form of error in believing Archimago just a few stanzas later. In defeating the monster Error, Redcrosse gains a certain confidence in his own abilities—a confidence that we soon learn is entirely unwarranted, for he falls prey to the very worst type of error, accepting hypocrisy as truth. But we can fall prey to precisely the same flaw if we fail to recognize Archimago for what he is. In effect, if we are to learn from the poem, we must recognize very early on what so few of the heroes learn until near the end of their adventures: overcoming the obvious manifestation of a vice does not mean that one has actually overcome that vice; rather, it merely means that one is capable of recognizing it in its most blatant forms. Recognizing the more subtle manifestations is the real test of virtue and the quality Spenser wants his readers to develop. This, in fact, seems to me to be Spenser's main aim in *The Faerie Queene*. Spenser is continually tempting us to fall by portraying sin not as just acceptable, but as almost overwhelmingly attractive. At the same time, we learn how to avoid falling prey to even the most attractive and appealing of vices, so that by the end of the poem, the reader is fully fashioned into that "vertuous and gentle discipline" Spenser sets as his goal.

THE ROLE OF PRINCE ARTHUR

While *The Faerie Queene* has a great many heroic figures—one or more for each book—the most heroic of all is Prince Arthur, the man destined to become the king who will unite all England and, not coincidentally, provide the great mythology that informs so much of British literary history. With the exception of Book III, Arthur intervenes in each book a number of times corresponding to the book number: once in Book I, twice in Book II, and so forth. He serves no such role in Book III, but that book has his female counterpart, Britomart. It seems fairly clear that had Spenser completed all of the projected 12 books, Arthur would have been the major figure of Book XII and would have taken part in 12 episodes. The culminating figure, then, would have been Prince Arthur, progenitor of the Tudor monarchy and the very figure of Magnificence, that most comprehensive of virtues: "So in the person of Prince Arthure I sette forth magnificence in particular, which vertue for that . . . it is the perfection of all the rest, and conteineth in it them all." More important, in coming to the aid of the various heroes at crucial moments, Arthur represents God's Grace, for it is, Spenser clearly believed, God's Grace that must save us. Our own effort alone is insufficient. And thus it is Arthur, the manifestation of Grace, who must intercede at crucial moments to save the heroes from impending and everlasting doom. In this respect, of course, we could consider Arthur the central figure of the poem, but that would be to reduce him to a mere formula, and thus diminish our enjoyment of the rich variety and puzzling complexity of the poem.

5

Book I:
The Legend of Holiness

Book I has long been the most popular section of *The Faerie Queene,* and for good reason. It is self-contained and hence easily detached from the remainder of the poem to be read (and anthologized) as a unit complete in itself. No cumbersome footnotes are needed to explain what events have occurred or how the characters have come to be where they are. Moreover, and perhaps most important, on the surface at any rate the narrative is clear, easily understood, enjoyable, exciting. Even young children can appreciate and enjoy this adventure tale about a young knight who aids a damsel in distress by saving her parents from the clutches of a horrific dragon. And along the way we meet characters almost guaranteed to hold our attention and captivate our fancy: the serpent Error and her carnivorous offspring; the wily hypocritical magician Archimago; the fierce brothers Sansjoy, Sansloy, and Sansfoy; the falsely beautiful witch Duessa and her giant lover Orgoglio; and assorted satyrs, knights, and lions (both fierce and protective). What more could we ask for in an adventure story?

Spenser gives us much more, though, for beneath the surface of this medieval tale of knights and ladies, courts and forests, dragons and magicians, he presents us with a route to our own salvation, to better knowledge of ourselves and a more thorough understanding of others. Book I is not just a graphic representation of the education of the Redcrosse Knight, or even of the Christian Knight; it also educates the reader. It is not just about learning to be holy, but also about learning not to be deceived.

The very first stanza of canto i provides us with a good sense of Spenser's methods and some indications of the sort of reading Book I requires:

> A Gentle Knight was pricking on the plaine,
>> Y cladd in mightie armes and siluer shielde,
>> Wherein old dints of deepe wounds did remaine,
>> The cruell markes of many' a bloudy fielde;
>> Yet armes till that time did he neuer wield:
>> His angry steede did chide his foming bitt,
>> As much disdayning to the curbe to yield:
>> Full iolly knight he seemd, and faire did sitt,
> As one for knightly giusts and fierce encounters fitt.

This stanza sets up a series of contrasts between what appears to be and what is. In it Spenser establishes, then violates, our expectations about this young knight. The first four lines seem to establish an unequivocally heroic figure: a "Gentle Knight" with "mightie armes and siluer shielde," a man tested in battle, as we can see by the "old dints of deepe wounds" on his shield and armor. He has been, we would assume from this description, in "many' a bloudy fielde." But line five makes clear that he is not at all what he seems: "Yet armes till that time did he neuer wield." He may be wearing the armor of an experienced and glamorous knight, carrying a battle-scarred shield, but he is himself full inexperienced, an untested, untried amateur.

The message in this opening stanza should be clear: things are not what they seem. In this poem as in life we cannot trust mere appearances, for they may be at odds with reality and truth. But that is not the only message of this first stanza, for we are also forced to question how far we are to trust the narrator as well. Is he going to tell us the whole truth and nothing but the truth, or is he going to mislead us? Will he be omniscient, keeping us informed accurately about his characters' thoughts and motivations, or will he make us work out the truth for ourselves? How far will he go in misleading us—and how far must we go in ensuring that we read carefully enough that we are not misled?

The next three lines provide us with some indications about answers to those questions. Lines six and seven are used to describe a horse not fully under its rider's control. The horse, an "angry steede" is foaming at the bit and attempting to overcome the knight's "curbe." There is a genuine question of how much control the rider is capable of maintaining over his steed. Yet line eight seems to undercut that interpretation: "Full iolly knight he seemd, and faire did sitt." If, in fact, his horse is foaming, angry, resistant, then it is hardly accurate to say that he sits "faire," as if he is an accomplished horseman. In fact, not until Book II and the fully reprehensible Braggadochio are we going to find a rider less capable of handling a horse.

In short, then, we are in danger of being misled by the narrator's remarks, and in attempting to mislead us, Spenser is also inviting our full participation in the poem. To reap the greatest rewards from this poem, we cannot be merely passive readers; rather, we must be actively engaged in coming to our own conclusions about events and characters, trusting no one, not even the narrator, to have a judgment surpassing our own. The true gentle and noble persons, those ideal readers for whom Spenser is writing, must learn to trust their own judgment, to reach conclusions based upon often contradictory, incomplete, even misleading evidence. And if our conclusions are sometimes wrong, if we find ourselves having to reassess a character or the significance of an event, then we, the readers, are living the very education the Redcrosse Knight must undergo in this book, learning to recognize the distinctions between the way things seem and the way they really are.

The knight's first adventure, in fact, is a demonstration that he does not see the distinction between what is and what seems to be. In his fight with the dragonlike monster, Error, he thinks he wins a glorious victory; in fact, Una even assures him that he has: "Well worthy be you of that Armorie, / Wherein ye haue great glory wonne this day, / And proou'd your strength on a strong enimie" (I.i.27). We are led by her praise to believe that the Redcrosse Knight has defeated Error in the abstract and thus is free to go on to further adventures. But it is not quite that simple, and many readers are surprised to discover that the Redcrosse Knight so quickly falls prey to another form of error in the person of Archimago, the personification of hypocrisy, before this first canto has ended.

In fact, although he has defeated Error, the remainder of Redcrosse's adventures center on his falling prey to various manifestations of error. Over and again he fails to take the lessons previously taught and apply them to his present situation. His defeat of Error is not the glorious victory he believes it has been; rather, it is an easy one. Error may have appeared to him in the form of a dragon, but indeed she is not a ferocious dragon. Exposed and brought to battle, obvious manifestations of error are easily defeated, and those who think their defeat has been a glorious and final victory are doomed to fall prey to error in its more subtle manifestations. And that is precisely what happens to Redcrosse. He must learn that responding to the obvious challenges in life, defeating the obvious foes to well-being, is merely the first step in moral development.

His defeat of Error, though, sends Redcrosse not directly on the path to knowledge, but rather on one toward a dangerous and debilitating pride, a path that will end with his defeat at the hands of Orgoglio, the very manifestation of arrogant, martial and sexual pride. Redcrosse is not helped, unfortunately, by Una's encouraging words in the battle with Error. She tells him that he has won great glory, but he has insufficient experience and knowledge to temper that praise with humility, and he begins to trust too much in his own judgment. After all, he was warned by both Una and the Dwarf to beware the Cave of Error, yet he disregarded their warnings and emerged victorious, which he takes as a sign that his own judgment is sufficient. Indeed, to him

Archimago is merely the "aged Sire" he appears to be when they meet, and the false sprites Archimago summons forth to portray a lascivious Una and her lover seem fully real. The young knight's emotions and wounded pride cloud whatever of his common sense he has left, and Archimago succeeds in separating him from Una, sending the Knight further on his downward path and leaving his lady without the armed protection she requires.

Believing himself to be morally superior to Una and forgetting his sworn duties altogether, Redcrosse abandons his quest and his lady to set out on his own in search of adventure, and much to his eventual dismay, he finds adventures soon enough. He is accompanied on his travels by Una's Dwarf, who seems to have abandoned his mistress for no apparent reason. If, however, we take the Dwarf to represent "common sense," it is clear that Redcrosse has far more need of him than Una, for he is totally without common sense of his own. Allegorical consistency may require the Dwarf to stay with the knight until he is no longer needed, when he may, like King Lear's Fool, simply fade from sight.

Having fallen prey to irrational jealousy in seeing the false Una and her paramour, Redcrosse is ripe to fall victim to another woman, one who will make him seem to be the very center of her attentions: Duessa, Archimago's ally and the personification of duplicity, as her name indicates. Again Redcrosse falls prey to appearances, flattery, and misleading attentions. He easily defeats Duessa's companion, Sansfoy, and becomes the protector of "Fidessa," abandoning the perfection of Una for the more seductive charms of a well-disguised witch. He fully believes her woeful tale of being Sansfoy's captive, and never looks below the surface of her remarks on her parentage. In his dealings with Una, his judgment was overcome by his jealous rage; here it seems to be overcome by Duessa's flattery.

Failing entirely to see the parallels between the man-tree Fradubio's tale and his own situation, Redcrosse continues his descent into prideful behavior by accompanying Duessa to the House of Pride, a court obedient to the manifestation of ostentatious pride, Lucifera, daughter of Pluto and Proserpina. Here we think Redcrosse will surely learn the lesson he needs, for pride hardly comes in more obvious forms than those he encounters in this palace. Even the building itself provides powerful clues to its nature with its mortarless brick, gilded exterior, and sand foundation. But Redcrosse lets these details pass without notice, more intent upon what he sees as his insufficient reception in this glorious court. Even in recognizing the prideful behavior of the other denizens of the court, he still fails to recognize their faults in himself:

> Goodly they all that knight do entertaine,
>> Right glad with him to haue increast their crew;
>> But to *Duess'* each one himselfe did paine
>> All kindnesse and faire courtesie to shew;
>> For in that court whylome her well they knew:
>> Yet the stout Faerie mongst the middest crowd
>> Thought all their glorie vaine in knightly vew,
>> And that great Princess too exceeding prowd,
> That to strange knight no better countenance allowd.
>
> (I.iv.15)

Redcrosse's adventure at the House of Pride is one of the great allegorical set pieces of the poem, the parade of Lucifera and her six counselors in canto iv. Spenser creates in this parade of the seven deadly sins a pictorial scene, a tableau that in his advanced state of pride the Redcrosse Knight does not seem fully to comprehend. One has, in fact, little sense of the knight's even watching this parade; it is there for us, the readers, not for him, and it is there less to edify than merely to entertain, to present a portrait of sin in all its various colorful and obvious manifestations.

The portrait is allegorical, to be sure, but these figures never really become part of the poem. They are less characters than mere personified abstractions, and they no more enter the action of the poem than a painting hanging on the wall. Their purpose is to illustrate for us (and for the unwitting Redcrosse Knight) where sin will lead us (and him), for each of Lucifera's counselors rides upon a particularly significant beast, wears appropriate clothing, and suffers from diseases or disorders associated with that vice. They ride upon a slothful ass (Idleness), a filthy swine (Gluttony), a bearded goat (Lechery), a camel laden with gold (Avarice), a ravenous wolf (Envy), and a vicious lion (Wrath). Idleness suffers from a "shaking feuer," perhaps indicating a muscular degeneration from lack of exercise similar to that which affects many victims of Parkinson's disease. Gluttony suffers a "dry dropsie," a condition brought about by excessive drink, which leads to dropsy (an accumulation of liquids in the body's cells), which, in turn, leads to excessive thirst. Lechery suffers from "that fowle euill, which all men reproue, / That rots the marrow, and consumes the braine," syphilis, the obvious disease for one overindulgent in sexual pleasures. Avarice suffers from gout, a disorder caused by indulgence in excessively rich foods, which torments him "eke in foote and hand" so that he can stand to touch nothing. Envy suffers from leprosy, or at the very least is said to have a "leprous mouth" from which he spews forth poisonous remarks about everyone (especially poets). Wrath suffers from a plethora of diseases associated with intemperance: "The swelling Splene, and Frenzy raging rife, / The shaking Palsey, and Saint *Fraunces* fire."

The allegorical portrait that Spenser presents to us with these counselors is meant to strike the mind's eye, to stand before us as an image that illustrates for us vice in its most horrid forms. But we do not learn from that image; rather we, like Redcrosse, must not be fooled into thinking we understand vice merely because we recognize its obvious manifestations. We must learn to overcome its subtle forms as well. And, of course, Redcrosse does not. He is not taken in by all this, striking though it may be; he is only barely attendant upon the ceremonies.

With the entry of Sansjoy, Redcrosse agrees to armed combat over the shield he earlier won from Sansfoy, a combat that centers on a question of pride: Sansjoy's familial pride, his need to avenge his brother's death and maintain the family honor, and Redcrosse's pride in having defeated Sansfoy and thus having won the shield, a prize he fully intends to retain.

In this battle, the narrator tells us—not once, but in the first line of two successive stanzas—"th' one for wrong, the other striues for right" (I.v.8 and 9), but it isn't entirely clear which is which. Redcrosse has by now fallen so far to pride that before the battle his primary concentration is on how victory will increase his glory, as the opening of canto v makes clear:

> The noble hart, that harbours vertuous thought,
>   And is with child of glorious great intent,
>   Can neuer rest, vntill it forth haue brought
>   Th' eternall brood of glorie excellent:
>   Such restlesse passion did all night torment
>   The flaming corage of that Faery knight,
>   Deuizing, how that doughtie turnament
>   With greatest honour he atchieuen might;
> Still did he wake, and still did watch for dawning light.
>   (I.v.1)

Given the situation, Redcrosse can hardly be said at this point to have a "noble hart"; the implicit praise of the first four lines, then, may apply to him only ironically, if at all. The "restlesse passion" that informs him through the night surely is not the passion of the virtuous, nor is he able to sleep the sleep of the innocent before his battle. During the fight, when Duessa calls out to Sansjoy, "Thine the shield, and I, and all" (I.v.11), Redcrosse mistakenly believes the promise is for him and, reacting as he did to Una's encouraging calls in the battle with Error, is inspired to greater effort and victory. Only Duessa's magical intervention saves Sansjoy from certain destruction—and, incidentally, Redcrosse from unjustly killing a man for entirely wrongheaded reasons.

Redcrosse is not, however, saved from falling victim to the appeals of this court and swearing obedience to Lucifera, thus continuing his downward spiral by committing himself consciously and verbally to the service of Pride, forgetting entirely his sworn obeisance to Gloriana and his duty to Una. His escape from the House of Pride comes through no insight of his own, but rather only at the urging of the Dwarf, who has seen the horrors awaiting them in the dungeon and who persuades him to leave. The opening of the next canto, in fact, strongly implies that Redcrosse has escaped damnation only by accident:

> As when a ship, that flyes faire vnder saile,
>   An hidden rocke escaped hath vnwares,
>   That lay in waite her wrack for to bewaile,
>   The Marriner yet halfe amazed stares
>   At perill past, and yet in doubt ne dares
>   To ioy at his foole-happie ouersight:
>   So doubly distrest twixt ioy and cares
>   The dreadless courage of this Elfin knight,
> Hauing escapt so sad ensamples in his sight.
>   (I.vi.1)

Saved from the horrid inhabitants of the House of Pride by the Dwarf's grizzly discovery of the corpses in the palace dungeon, Redcrosse once more abandons a woman to whom he has committed himself to continue on his own aimless way. He has no quest, no companion save the Dwarf, and no apparent goals for himself other than to roam the countryside waiting for something to happen. And something does when Duessa catches up with him and leads him further down the path to his own destruction. Even with his escape, he is still in the thrall of Duessa and regrets "that his too hastie speed / The faire *Duess'* had forst him leaue behind" (I.v.2).

One would expect that the Redcrosse Knight would be wary of the woman who had led him to the Palace of Pride, but he naively makes no connection between her and the dangers he faced there. Rather, he greets her without suspicion, accepts her readily as his traveling companion, and soon falls prey to her sexual charms and victim to the debilitating effects of the well to which she leads him. When he removes his armor and drinks the soporific waters of the well, Redcrosse's fate is settled—and appears in the form of Orgoglio, Duessa's true lover, the son of Aeolus and Earth and the manifestation of sexual pride. Orgoglio's very name ("swollen with pride") in fact carries sexual connotations, as Shakespeare well knew when he referred to "the Princes orgulous" who come to Troy to recapture Helen.[22] It is this sexual pride which at last leads to Redcrosse's downfall, for in his soporific state, he is easily seduced by Duessa, defeated by Orgoglio, and tossed deep into a dungeon guarded by the backward-looking Ignaro.

He has not just been overcome by a huge and strong enemy, but rather has fallen to his own ever-increasing pride, pride that begins with his borrowed, unearned armor and continues throughout his adventures; pride in his martial prowess in defeating Error; pride in his moral superiority in abandoning the lascivious image of Una; pride in his appearance and glory at Lucifera's palace; and finally sexual pride in his encounter with Duessa. Now the Redcrosse Knight's only hope is God's Grace, which will soon arrive in the form of Prince Arthur.

Thus far we have entirely ignored Una except as Redcrosse's companion very early in the Book. But she has a set of adventures of her own, although they are more akin to allegorical set pieces than to the series of causally linked events Redcrosse experiences. Separated from Redcrosse, she is left to her own devices, but without him she has insufficient protection and thus is very much at risk, particularly pursued as she is by Archimago, her archenemy (for, on the allegorical level, Hypocrisy, which he represents, hates Truth, which she represents).

By the end of canto i, thanks to the efforts of the wily Archimago, Una and Redcrosse are separated, not to be reunited again until canto vii, when she brings Prince Arthur to rescue him from Orgoglio's dungeon. Between the separation and the reunion, our major focus is on the Redcrosse Knight and his adventures, but Spenser also draws us back regularly to Una and the various dangers she must face. Many readers, particularly those in their first experience with the poem, complain that Una is as one-dimensional as her name would suggest, a character with neither development nor particular motivation, who wanders through the book in search of her protector, coming under the protection of and falling prey to those who only coincidentally cross her path. Indeed, her development as a character is at best limited, and her only true actions (besides guiding Redcrosse) seem to be in snatching Despaire's knife from Redcrosse's hand in canto ix. But in snatching that knife from Redcrosse's hand, she saves his life, and in guiding Redcrosse from Orgoglio's dungeon to Caelia's House of Holiness, she saves his soul.

Nonetheless, she is a character of a different nature from Redcrosse, and her allegorical significance as Truth, or the True Church, does not permit for the sort of development we see in her companion. The Christian Knight must develop, must learn how to react and how to behave. His is an experience we can emulate. But Truth is absolute, subject to danger to be sure, but not to development; what development there is must come in the ways we perceive Truth, not in the truth itself. Redcrosse must learn to recognize Una for what she is, but it is he who must change, not she.

This essentially one-dimensional characterization, based upon her allegorical significance, does not, however, prevent Una from having interesting adventures and from encountering friends and foes who hold our attention more than she can by herself. Archimago is her primary foe, as hypocrisy always seeks to undermine truth. But he cannot himself harm her; rather he must separate her from her protectors and thus leave her open to harm by other, more active, vices. Thus she is prey to the essentially harmless (and rather amusing) Abessa and Corceca ("Blind Devotion"), their more sinister companion Kirkrapine ("raper of churches"), and the far more dangerous Sansloy ("lawlessness"), third of the Sans-brothers who threaten Redcrosse and Una throughout the early cantos of Book I. At the same time, however, she is aided by a fearless lion who recognizes her virginal qualities and thus will not harm her, a tribe of savage but essentially harmless Satyrs who want to worship her as a pagan idol, and Sir Satyrane, half-man, half-satyr, who rescues her from the Satyrs, then sets off in search of Sansloy.

Viewing all this in its most simplistic allegorical terms, we can see that militant—and protestant—Christianity (the Redcrosse Knight), separated from Truth (Una), will fall prey to the duplicity and pride of the Roman Catholic Church (personified by Duessa, daughter of the Pope), while Truth, lead astray by Hypocrisy (Archimago), will be endangered by lawlessness (Sansloy) and those who would destroy the churches (Kirkrapine), or be relegated to the wilderness represented by the tribe of Satyrs. Only God's Grace (Prince Arthur) can intervene to bring militant Christianity and Truth together.

But there is more to the poem than such simple allegory. Una's adventures, which occupy cantos iii and vi, serve as a respite for the reader from Redcrosse's more complex events in cantos ii, iv, and v and demonstrate that others see what Redcrosse does not: the value of Truth in the form of Una.

In intermingling their adventures Spenser is also able to maintain a level of suspense, breaking off one narrative at a crucial moment to concentrate on the other. Thus he shifts our focus from one character to the other, keeping them separate yet connected and anticipating their reunion at the end of canto vii, when Redcrosse will come under the guidance and protection of Una, their roles reversed as a result of his moral insufficiencies.

At each step of his early adventures occupying the first half of Book I, the Redcrosse Knight defeats an obvious manifestation of vice only to fall prey, sometimes immediately, to the same vice in a far subtler form. His defeat of Error, as we have seen, is followed directly by his encounter with Archimago. The same sort of thing happens to Redcrosse when he defeats Sansfoy, faithlessness, and immediately falls under the spell of Duessa. He has overcome a relatively obvious manifestation of faithlessness, but has fallen prey to a woman who is the very antithesis of the true faith, emblematically the Whore of Babylon and daughter of the hated Pope, "He that the wide West under his rule has / And hath high set his throne where *Tiberis* doth pas" (I.ii.22). And fleeing indignantly from the false, lascivious Una conjured up by Archimago, Redcrosse encounters Duessa, the woman whose lust will lead to his total downfall in canto vii.

The first half of Book I, then, is concerned primarily with Redcrosse's fall from grace, his descent into pride. The second half is concerned largely with his salvation, his movement from being a defeated, despairing knight to being the savior of Una's parents and homeland—and eventually becoming St. George, patron saint of England. The knight's movement in the first half of the book was toward solitude and an unreliable self-dependence based upon a faulty view of his own physical, intellectual, and moral powers; in the second half he moves toward community and a self-reliance based upon his newly secured faith in himself and in God. The first step toward that community and self-reliance is his rescue from Orgoglio's dungeon by Prince Arthur, whom Una has recently encountered during her separate adventures.

Arthur and his squire (who we much later learn is named Timias) defeat Orgoglio and Duessa and release Redcrosse from the dungeon after a three-month captivity. Spenser's portrayal of the rescued Redcrosse Knight is a masterly bit of psychological realism. His eyes sunken, his body gaunt and defeated, squinting into the sunlight, Redcrosse stands silently in the presence of his rescuers, too ashamed of his fall even to speak, especially in the presence of Una, whom by now he must surely realize he has so badly wronged.

After an exchange of gifts, Arthur goes on his way, leaving Una to accompany Redcrosse to the House of Holiness, where he will be cured. But having fallen so far, having suffered from so much pride and now realizing his faults, Redcrosse must first face still another dreadful enemy: Despaire and the temptation to suicide.

In the Cave of Despaire, Spenser presents a bit of psychological realism and a portrait not just of despair, but of the dangers of false logic as well. Having fallen as far as he has, recognizing his own insufficiencies and his betrayal of his duty, Redcrosse is deeply ashamed, in despair, and thus his visit to the Cave of Despaire is consistent with human experience. There Despaire sermonizes him, convincing him of his sinfulness and that, should he go on living, he will only continue to sin more and more. The arguments Despaire presents are powerful and moving, and the reader, like Redcrosse, is in danger of accepting their logic. But Una, Truth, saves Redcrosse at the crucial moment, not just by snatching the knife with which he means to commit suicide from his hand, but by reminding him of that ultimate saving feature of his religion—God's Grace: "In heauenly mercies hast thou not a part? / Why shouldst thou then despeire, that chosen art?" (I.ix.53).

Saved from himself, Redcrosse is not cured, but he is at least now ready for purgation of his sins, and for that he must journey with Una to the House of Holiness, where he will be treated and cured under the direction of a mother, Caelia (Heavenliness), and her three daughters, Fidelia, Speranza, and Charissa (Faith, Hope, and Charity). Once he has been thoroughly prepared, he is led to the Holy Hospital where seven holy beadsmen minister to him, then to Holy Contemplation, who leads him to a vision of the New Jerusalem. Each step of this cure, his route to recovery in the second half of Book I, parallels a step in his fall in the first half. Arthur reunites Redcrosse and Una as Archimago had separated them; Una leads Redcrosse on the right and righteous path as Duessa had led him astray. The House of Holiness and its mistress Caelia parallel the House of Pride and Lucifera; the Seven Holy Beadsmen parallel the parade of the Seven Deadly Sins. And Redcrosse's fall into Orgoglio's dungeon, the final step of his path away from grace, is paralleled by his climb up the Mount of Contemplation where he sees a vision of the new Jerusalem and of his own glorious future as St. George. This episode, often referred to as the "allegorical center" of Book I, is crucial to our understanding of the Redcrosse Knight's significance as St. George of England and to the religious allegory of his book. At the same time, however, it is also often seen as less than fully satisfactory by first-time readers of the poem, for it is essentially static; the allegorical level of the poem seems to subsume the narrative, religious signification becoming here not just important, but the overriding element. Modern readers are also often troubled that in order to understand the events of this episode, they must resort more often than they wish to the footnotes.

Nonetheless, the Redcrosse Knight's cure at the House of Holiness and the Holy Hospital, his vision of the New Jerusalem, and his new-found knowledge that he is in fact St. George of England and not a Faery knight are all crucial elements to our full understanding of the book's significance. And if we grow impatient with their presentation, assuming a greater knowledge than we have, perhaps we have not fully learned the lesson Redcrosse has been taught. The true path to salvation is not thrilling and exciting in itself. The House of Pride may be more entertaining for the reader, but during Redcrosse's cure we learn the unadorned truth of how salvation is achieved.

Having been cured both physically and morally, Redcrosse is now ready to accomplish the task he was assigned before we saw him in canto i, the rescue of Una's homeland from the horrible fire-breathing dragon, a battle Spenser describes in careful detail. The inexperienced youth of canto i, bumbling his way from disaster to disaster, is now ready for the ultimate test of his courage and faith, and just as his first battle was with a dragon, so is his last, but this dragon is different. Before his fall, before his salvation, he was certainly no match for the dragon he must face for Una. Error may have frightened him, but she presented no real threat; even her offspring were little more than troublesome gnats. This dragon, however, is quite real, strong, brave, ferocious—and yet Redcrosse, strengthened by his faith, defeats it after a three-day battle. It is significant that the victory takes three days and that the first two days are so difficult for the knight. At the end of the first day, Redcrosse is nearly killed and left at sundown near the Well of Life, which revives him for the second day's battle. The saving graces of the Well of Life recall not only Fradubio's lament in canto ii that he and Fraelissa can be saved only by the waters of a living well, but also the enchanted waters Duessa gives Redcrosse immediately before his defeat by Orgoglio. The second day's battle ends when Redcrosse is knocked down and falls under the Tree of Life, a parallel to Fradubio himself and to the giant oak Orgoglio uses as his club, which so nearly becomes the tree of death for Redcrosse. On the third day, Redcrosse arises with the accumulated benefits of baptism and communion gained from the Well and the Tree of Life and quickly, almost unceremoniously, dispatches the dragon, saving Una and her parents (whom we realize allegorically are Adam and Eve—and thus representative of all humanity). Redcrosse has, at last, been victorious over the forces of death.

But that is not the end, for Archimago still roams free and would still seem to be a threat to Una and Redcrosse. Spenser must, however, demonstrate that his threat is now more apparent than real, and when Archimago arrives (in disguise) at the betrothal ceremonies to announce that Redcrosse is already betrothed to "Fidessa," Redcrosse readily recognizes and unmasks him, sending him off to imprisonment. The Redcrosse Knight demonstrates that, from his adventures, his near death, and his salvation by God's grace and good works, he has learned at last the difference between appearance and reality and will not fall victim to hypocrisy. Lest we think that we are safe and well, though, Spenser lets us know that Archimago will somehow escape—and we will soon meet him in Book II.

6

Book II:
The Legend of Temperance

Like the first book, Book II deals with the self-contained adventures of a single hero, set forth in a relatively straightforward, although episodic, narrative. The opening of Book II requires some knowledge of Book I—both the Redcrosse Knight and Archimago make early appearances—and there are some other characters who later reappear from the first book, but it is not long before the new hero, Sir Guyon, and his companion, the mysterious Palmer, are off on entirely new, independent adventures, unrelated (on the level of the narrative, at least) to the events of Book I. While it would clearly violate Spenser's intentions for the poem, one could read Book II in isolation from Book I and from the books that follow. In point of fact, though, few readers do.

The proem to Book II opens with reference to the poem as "this famous antique history," reminding us that Spenser earlier called upon Clio, the Muse of History, to aid him in his task. The poet remarks in the proem that some will consider what he has to say a "painted forgery, / Rather then matter of iust memory." The remarks on history and memory are especially significant for this book, particularly in light of the episode in the Chamber of Memory in Alma's castle in canto x. Furthermore, Spenser here makes use of contemporary events to stress that his fiction may be no stranger than the discovery of Peru or the Amazon River or Virginia—or even the current theory that there are other worlds, like the earth, circling other stars.

In Book II, as in Book I, we can see Spenser's original conception for *The Faerie Queene* still intact: a single hero undergoes several adventures, is eventually separated from his companion, falls prey to a powerful enemy, and is debilitated. His companion returns and, with the aid of Prince Arthur, the hero is rescued. Arthur and the companion take the hero to a place of rehabilitation from which he can complete his quest without further ado. By Book III, as we shall see, Spenser's plan falters, his mode of operation changes, but there is a consistency between Books I and II sufficient to suggest that they were written fairly close together and with a clear, unwavering plan in mind. Whatever Spenser came to think of as his master plan for the later books, Books I and II are clearly parallel in structure and intent.

Spenser's intention was to educate the "gentleman or noble person," and he clearly planned this book to be the second stage of that education, for having learned the virtue of holiness, the reader is now ready to be schooled in the virtue of temperance. As many have observed, each book builds upon its predecessors. Book II, then, is as much a preparation for further adventures as Book I, for the heroes Spenser portrays in subsequent books must be possessed not only of holiness, but of temperance as well. As Maurice Evans points out, "Britomart [in Books III and IV] has to steer her way between virginity and lust; Artegall [in Book V] between the letter of the law and indiscriminate mercy; Calidore [in Book VI] between idealism and the claims of the real. Each of Spenser's virtues is itself a specific Golden Mean."[23]

The very nature of temperance presents some interesting problems for the reader as well as for Sir Guyon. The road to holiness is—or at least should be—fairly straight and narrow; the Redcrosse Knight's problem is that he is distracted from it, led on other byways to his near destruction. But once he has found his way, his progress, although painful, is inexorable, and having achieved holiness he need pursue it no further. He has reached a state of being rather than of behaving, and all he must do is maintain that state. Once one accepts such holiness, one possesses it fully and eternally unless one actively rejects or disregards it.

Redcrosse's education, while varied, is rather straightforward, narrative in structure; his goal is clear from the beginning of his quest, for there is a broadly accepted and relatively clear definition of holiness to which he must adhere if he is to succeed. But temperance is quite another matter. Once one achieves holiness the temptations to abandon the virtue are considerable but relatively easily overcome. But even the holiest can fall prey to intemperance. After all, even excessive attention to the contemplative life can be a form of intemperance. Merely recognizing the necessities of the Christian life and abiding by them would not be sufficient for the gentleman or noble person Spenser says he hopes to educate with *The Faerie Queene*.

The next step toward such perfection is, in fact, temperance. It is important for us to recognize that Guyon represents temperance from the beginning of Book II. Redcrosse must learn to *become* holy; Guyon must learn to *maintain* temperance. In the last stanza of the proem, Spenser asks that his reader

> vouchsafe with patient eare
> The braue aduentures of this Faery knight,
> The good Sir *Guyon*, gratiously to heare,
> In whom great rule of Temp'raunce goodly doth appear.

As the last line indicates, Guyon already possesses temperance; he must maintain it in this book.

In moving from Book I to Book II, we move from the world of faith to the secular world. Redcrosse is shown a heavenly vision in Book I: the New Jerusalem; Guyon is shown an earthly vision in Book II: the Briton and Elfin Chronicles. Redcrosse is shown the future,

Guyon the past, while both are rooted in the present: one is shown where he is going, the other from whence he came. Redcrosse's fate is unequivocal: he is to become St. George, Patron Saint of England; that much he learns from his vision. Guyon's vision is less clear—and certainly less prophetic: he learns only that Faerie Land has a history and that the history of Britain is marked by the upward and downward currents of temperate and intemperate behavior among its monarchs. Redcrosse's duty is to fulfill his vision; Guyon's duty is to maintain his heritage. This distinction between becoming and being is an important one for an adequate understanding of Book II. Guyon's quest is one of maintaining continuity with his history, both as a Faery knight and as an individual striving to maintain the Golden Mean in all his forms of behavior. The holiness Redcrosse must learn is a revealed trait; the temperance Guyon must maintain can be learned only by observing the behavior of others and consciously seeking out the Golden Mean.

By the seventh stanza of the Book we learn that Guyon controls his horse to match its pace with that of the Palmer—an emblem, perhaps, of his ability to control himself as well as his steed. It is, surely, a contrast to our first view of Redcrosse, who was unable to control his horse, and it will later contrast with Braggadochio (in canto iii), whose lack of horsemanship is an emblem of his own unknightly characteristics.

Unlike the Redcrosse Knight, Guyon does not undergo a series of causally linked adventures leading first to his downfall, then to his rebirth and regeneration (although his "faint" upon leaving the Cave of Mammon can certainly be interpreted in these very terms). Each of the Redcrosse Knight's adventures leads directly—and causally—to the next, but not so with Guyon's. He is presented with a series of exempla, and the process of education, more for the reader than for the hero, is cumulative rather than causal, and leads to Spenser's challenge to the reader (but not to Guyon) in the final, climactic event, the destruction of the Bowre of Bliss.

But before considering that event, we should consider the concept of temperance and how Spenser means for us to understand it. Many first-time readers are struck by what they take to be the inconsistencies of Guyon's behavior, his participation in battles, his anger, his sorrow, as if those qualities were the very ones he must learn to overcome. For such readers, Guyon never seems to learn the lessons of the book, for at the end he destroys the Bowre in what appears to be almost a frenzy. But temperance as Spenser and the Renaissance understood it does not mean abstinence or total and absolute control of one's emotions; rather, in its simplest terms, it is that Renaissance ideal of behavior, the Golden Mean, a midpoint between pure contemplative indolence and rash, unconsidered action. It is not, nor should it be construed to be, inaction or abstinence from all forms of pleasure. A total rejection of earthly things is as much an act of intemperance as an indiscriminate acceptance of them.

Temperance may best be illustrated by the Medina episode of canto ii. Setting off with the Palmer after their discovery of Ruddymane, Guyon comes upon a castle occupied by three sisters, "the children of one sire by mothers three" (II.ii.13). These sisters represent three stages of being: deficiency (Elissa, the oldest), excess (Perissa, the youngest), and the mean (Medina, the middle sister). They may, at the allegorical level, have any number of significances: moral, sensual, religious, perhaps even political. Medina is clearly the best of the three; she "did far excell / The other two," the narrator tells us at stanza 14. Neither excess nor deficiency is acceptable, but rather a balance of the two is most desirable.

The companions of Elissa and Perissa may also illustrate the two extremes Guyon must strive to keep in balance within himself. Elissa is accompanied by Sir Huddibras, "an hardy man; / Yet not so good of deedes as great of name" (II.ii.17); his reputation clearly exceeds him. He is "more huge in strength, then wise in workes," and "foolehardize" overcomes his reason, "sterne melancholy" his "courage." His armor, "for terrour more," has the appearance of gold without the substance, for it is mere "shyning bras," befitting one of his name. A more suitable companion for deficiency we could hardly find. Perissa's companion is a villain we have seen before, Sansloy, "the most vnruly, and the boldest boy / That euer warlike weapons menaged" (II.ii.18). But his boldness is not a point of praise, for it is boldness without compassion; he cares not who he "bereau'd of right" or "endamaged." His actions as Una's adversary in Book I should have made those characteristics clear enough, but his consorting with Perissa makes them unequivocal.

Medina is unaccompanied and may accept Guyon, Temperance himself, as her temporary and fitting companion, thus completing the three sets of two. But the other two knights are unable to control their tempers; they see Guyon and each other as threats and are quick to spring to action. A furious battle ensues and Guyon, at first a mere observer, is drawn into it, while Elissa and Perissa urge their knights on and Medina calls for concord. Medina prevails, and, for the moment at least, temperate behavior rules and dinner may proceed. The middle sister, lest we miss the point, is seated between her intemperate siblings and brings peace to the household. The allegory of this passage may be essentially naive, the "message" only too clear, but it nonetheless helps us better understand the role Guyon must seek to play throughout the remainder of the book. His will be a role balanced between extremes, striving always for the Golden Mean against the equal pulls of excess and deficiency.

We should not, however, be misled into believing that Guyon is without fault and that he has nothing to learn from his adventures. There is progress in this book and in his behavior, and although he may be generally temperate, he is certainly not above reproach. In fact, the lessons of Book II are learned through the series of temptations Guyon must face and overcome, and while his adventures are less dramatic than those of the Redcrosse Knight, they are no less important for his—and our—education. Temperance is a more subtle and complex virtue than holiness, and that subtlety and complexity are reflected in Guyon's adventures.

Book I is devoted to single characters and single foes. Redcrosse and Una belong together, but they are separated, and both face individual foes, or at least foes working essentially alone. When Redcrosse

and Una are reunited, the adventure may move toward closure. Book
II, on the other hand, focuses on Guyon, with far less attention to the
Palmer as companion. It never focuses on the Palmer alone. In the first
half of the book, we find several pairs of characters, all representative
in one way or another of extremes that Guyon must avoid if he is to
maintain the Golden Mean: Archimago and Duessa, Mordant and
Amavia, Braggadochio and Trompart, Elissa and Perissa, Huddibras
and Sansloy, Furor and Occasion, Pyrochles and Cymochles, Phedon
and Philomon (even though we never see the latter but only hear of
him). Guyon must even strike a balance between Mammon, the agent
of Satan, and Arthur, the agent of God.

Guyon is first tempted to action by Archimago and Duessa against
his ally, the Redcrosse Knight. But Guyon does not enter into battle
with Redcrosse. He has been told that Redcrosse is guilty of a most
heinous crime and prepares to fight "inflam'd with wrathfulnesse"
(II.i.25) as he approaches Redcrosse. But when he recognizes his adversary's armor and shield, Guyon lowers his lance and greets him in
friendship:

> Mercie Sir knight, and mercie Lord,
> For mine offence and heedlesse hardiment,
> That had almost committed crime abhord,
> And with reprochfull shame mine honour shent,
> Whiles cursed steele aginst that badge I bent,
> The sacred badge of my Redeemers death,
> Which on your shield is set for ornament:
> But his fierce foe his steede could stay vneath,
> Who prickt with courage kene, did cruell battell breath.
>
> (II.i.27)

He has been momentarily misled, but he can control himself already,
take into account what he knows both at first hand and by reputation
of his supposed foe, balance his own knowledge against what Archimago has told him, and reach a reasonable, temperate, conclusion. His
slip into angry vengefulness has been only temporary.

Having survived this temptation, he comes upon the dead Mordant, the dying Amavia, and their blood-splattered child, whom he will soon name "Ruddymane." Mordant and Amavia represent the results of two further types of intemperance: excess of guilt and grief, behavior we suspect Guyon will not fall victim to but which we need to be shown to help strengthen our own resolve. Mordant has fallen prey to sexual intemperance in Acrasia's Bowre of Bliss, then to his own guilt; Amavia has fallen prey to a misdirected and excessive grief, which has prompted her to suicide, leaving her child both unprotected and orphaned. Only the fortuitous approach of Guyon and the Palmer saves the child from being helplessly exposed to the elements and the beasts of the forest. But while Guyon can save the child, he cannot rid him of the sins of his parents. His mother's blood cannot be washed from his hands—and hence his name. The Palmer explains the inability of the water of the well to wash away the blood by relating an Ovidian tale of metamorphosis; several readers have suggested that the indelible blood is intended to remind us that baptism can preserve the soul, but that it does not in itself wash away all sin. However one chooses to interpret the episode, the blood on the child is a visible and permanent symbol of Amavia's and Mordant's intemperate behavior and its effects on their child's future.

It is this event that sends Guyon off on his quest, for he vows to destroy Acrasia's Bowre in order to avenge the deaths of Mordant and Amavia and prevent others from suffering a like fate. Guyon's impetus for this quest is very much at odds with Spenser's own account in his letter to Sir Walter Ralegh. That Spenser chose to begin with Guyon's encounter with Archimago and Redcrosse rather than with Ruddymane and the Palmer may indicate a desire to demonstrate clearly Guyon's already existent temperance rather than to produce another bildungsroman on the order of Book I.

In his rush to aid Amavia and Ruddymane, Guyon leaves his horse unguarded, an action that leads to the introduction of Braggadochio and Trompart, whose cowardly responses to each other and to Belphoebe provide a marvelously comic moment in this otherwise often somber book. There is more to their episode, though, than mere comic relief, for they represent still another form of intemperance, one Spenser could not portray in his hero without betraying his temperance: excessive and unwarranted pride. After all, if Guyon is to fall victim to pride, as Redcrosse does in Book I, then he can hardly maintain his temperance. Braggadochio, on the other hand, is

> One that to bountie neuer cast his mind,
> Ne thought of honour euer did assay
> His baser brest, but in his kestrell kind
> A pleasing vaine of glory vaine did find,
> To which his flowing toung, and troublous spright
> Gaue him great ayd, and made him more inclind.
>
> (II.iii.4)

Braggadochio's newfound companion, Trompart, is a perfect mate for him,

> For he was wylie witted, and growne old
> In cunning sleights and practick knauery.
> From that day forth he cast for to vphold
> His idle humour with fine flattery,
> And blow the bellowes to his swelling vanity.
>
> (II.iii.9)

In these two, Spenser shows us the comic underbelly of intemperance—they are a parodic Guyon and Palmer, the false knight a cowardly braggart dressed in unearned armor and riding a stolen horse, his companion a charlatan and sycophant, whose mere trickery and flattery parody the Palmer's magical powers and sage advice. In his attempts to emulate and praise a way of life he neither experiences nor understands and in his lustful advances on Belphoebe, Braggadochio demonstrates how foolish the intemperate may look. Sir Philip Sidney, Spenser's contemporary, observes that a "comedy is an imitation of the common errors of our life, which [the playwright] representeth, in the most ridiculous and scornful sort that may be, so as it is impossible that any beholder can be content to be such a one."[24] Surely this is the sort of thing Spenser has in mind for Braggadochio and Trompart: their foolish behavior is intended to remind us that we, too, stand in danger of looking foolish if we act as they do.

We have seen many similarities between Books I and II; however, there are many ways in which the techniques of the earlier book are reversed in Book II. In Book I we saw characters in action, then were given a characterization of them. We have, for example, more than enough evidence to identify Archimago as untrustworthy before we are told his real name and character. But Braggadochio is characterized very directly before we ever see him in action. We know what he is like and thus expect his comically foolish actions. Similarly, although Redcrosse must first meet and defeat obvious and blatant Error before he falls prey to error's more subtle forms, Guyon has already overcome furor in his approach to Redcrosse and learned the dangers of occasion in the fight in Medina's castle well before he encounters Furor and Occasion in canto iv. If the method of Book I is deductive, then that of Book II is inductive: Redcrosse is shown first the personified abstraction (e.g., Error), then the subtler manifestations of the vice represented by that abstraction; Guyon sees first the manifestations, then meets the personified abstractions. To achieve holiness, we could say, one is given "the word" and must accept conformity to it; to learn temperance, however, one must interpolate the principles through active involvement.

Furthermore, Book II also departs significantly from Book I in that there is only rarely any real sense of danger to its hero. While Guyon must face many dangers and opponents throughout his adventure, we sense that there is but little chance that he will fall prey to them, unlike the Redcrosse Knight, who seems to fall prey to every possible foe until his rescue by Arthur. Guyon faces various dangers so that we, the readers, will be aware of them and see how to deal with them ourselves. He faces his challenges, fights his foes, and overcomes his obstacles, but he seems nearly always well up to the task at hand.

When he wavers, it is but momentarily or (after his visit to Mammon's cave) as a result of physical human frailty rather than moral or intellectual deficiency.

Nonetheless, he must still face and overcome a great variety of obstacles to his well-being and goals, and each victory leads to a new challenge, quite unlike those that have come before. Thus, once he has overcome the furor generated by his own temper and learned to avoid occasions for dispute when possible, he must also learn to overcome the excessive pleasures of mirth and indolence, which he meets in the person of Phaedria at the Lake of Idleness.

Phaedria represents wanton idleness or unmeasured mirth and is the first of the temptations to enjoyment Guyon must face. His earlier temptations have been essentially unattractive and hence relatively easy to avoid, but now he must avoid the temptations often considered worthwhile: ease, wealth, power. Phaedria invites Guyon aboard her little boat and, before the Palmer can join them, sails off, hoping to seduce Guyon to inaction if he is unprotected by the severe Palmer. She is disappointed, for the Palmer is less Guyon's guide and protector than his companion and counselor. Guyon seems to be sufficient in himself to overcome such threats. On the allegorical level, however, Guyon does not at this point have the Palmer by his side because he must learn to spur himself to action. Idleness is a deficit, something missing; the Palmer's primary role has been to this point to help protect him from forms of excess.

Finally, Guyon demonstrates that despite his virtues, he still has something to learn about temperate behavior, for he follows Mammon into the cave. Having overcome furor (and Furor), ire (and Occasion), and wanton idleness (Phaedria), Guyon must now withstand the temptations of wealth offered to him by Mammon and the power of being wed to Mammon's daughter, Philoteme. But there is more than just power involved, for Philoteme's very name ("Love of Honor") indicates the sort of excess she represents. Guyon has potentially earned much honor for his exploits, and he will earn still more before the end of the book, but he must avoid the intemperate love of honor for its own sake and keep clearly in mind that honor accrues from good deeds and should spur one to further good deeds, not to pride in oneself.

Guyon has been criticized for going into Mammon's Cave, for exposing himself to such temptations; they are, after all, almost too much for him, for he falls into a deathlike swoon when he returns to the surface. On the other hand, his action has also been seen as heroic, likened to Christ's temptation in the wilderness. There is much to be said for both interpretations, but there is also a great deal of psychological realism in this episode: having rejected idleness and mirth in resisting Phaedria, Guyon must now overcome the temptation to work too hard at gathering wealth and false honor or power. He must, in other words, keep the pendulum from swinging too far in the other direction; he should not succumb to a life of meaningless leisure, nor should he become a workaholic. Spenser may well be pointing out that true temperance is so difficult to maintain that it places our very lives in danger and that Guyon, like the Redcrosse Knight, must ultimately depend upon God's grace for his survival after having fought his best fight and being overcome with his own human weaknesses.

And Guyon's weaknesses are indeed very human. His faint upon leaving Mammon's Cave no doubt has deep allegorical significance, but on a purely practical, human level (which, despite the allegory, Spenser is really never very far from), he has been in the Cave three days without rest, food, or water: he collapses in sheer exhaustion. The temptations of the world are so great and the flesh so weak that only God's grace (in the person of Arthur) can save him, then take him to the House of Alma where he learns his past—and hence his destiny— so he can go on, now fully resistant, and destroy the Bowre of Bliss.

It might not be too much of an exaggeration to say that the first eight cantos of Book II deal with the external enemies of temperance, while the last four deal with the internal enemies. This view can certainly be used to explain what happens within the Cave of Mammon and the House of Alma: Guyon manages to withstand all of the temptations of the earth and flesh, culminating in his three-day stay in the Cave of Mammon, where he successfully rejects the most tempting of all earthly pleasures—money, power, sex. Weak from his ordeal, he is taken to the House of Alma where, on the allegorical level, other temptations must be overcome—specifically, Spenser turns from external and controllable temptations to internal and inevitable temptations. The very body itself becomes intemperate—indeed incontinent (in the medical sense of that term) regardless of what we do. We will, perforce, grow old and ill. Only God's grace can save us from the despair of age and infirmity—and hence Arthur is necessary to save the House of Alma from the onslaughts of Maleger, the personification of age, debility, and disease. When old age and its infirmities attack us, we are defenseless without God's grace—i.e., Arthur.

That the Castle of Alma is an allegorical representation of the human body virtually goes without saying. The very first stanza of canto ix should leave no doubt:

> Of all Gods workes, which do this world adorne,
>> There is no one more faire and excellent,
>> Then is mans body both for powre and forme,
>> Whiles it is kept in sober gouernment;
>> But none then it, more fowle and indecent,
>> Distempred through misrule and passions bace:
>> It growes a Monster, and incontinent
>> Doth loose his dignitie and natiue grace.
> Behold, who list, both one and other in this place.
>
> (II.ix.1)

Alma's castle is, in fact, an almost grotesquely graphic representation of the human body, as even a casual reading of stanzas 21–32 makes clear. Since it is the site of Guyon's recovery, the Castle of Alma clearly parallels the House of Holiness in Book I. Like the House of Holiness episode, this section has also been considered the "allegorical center" of its book, for here we learn more not just of Faerie Land, but also of how the lessons of temperance apply directly to British history—and hence how Faerie Land and England are to be linked by the reader.

The Elfin chronicle, which Guyon reads in the room of Memory, is little more than a comical five stanza list, giving the genealogy of the Elfin monarchs: Elfe, Elfin, Elfinan, Elfiline, Elfinell, Elfant, Elfar, Elfinor, Elficleos, Elferon, and Oberon. But our real attention is on the book Arthur reads, the "chronicle of Briton kings" (II.x. headnote). Here we learn political temperance; we see how various incidents of political temperance and intemperance have led to the rise and fall of Britain at various times and come to recognize that the dangers of intemperance to the individual are minuscule indeed compared to the dangers of intemperance to a nation.

Again in this episode, Spenser departs significantly from his practice in Book I, for when Guyon leaves to continue his quest, Arthur remains—and our focus remains on him throughout canto xi, when he saves the castle from the attack of Maleger and his troops. For the first time, we see Arthur in a fully independent adventure.

Our attention in canto xii shifts back to Guyon and the Palmer, now on their way to Acrasia's Bowre, the ultimate goal of their quest. Illusory fears, both realistic and allegorical, attack them on their way—whirlpools, dangerous shoals, mermaids, unthriftiness, bankruptcy, sea monsters, blinding fog, birds, and bats—all conjured up by Acrasia (the Palmer tells Guyon) and all representing various forms of intemperate behavior and its dangers. Once ashore, they face still more monsters, but these, like the sea monsters, the Palmer quickly dispatches with his magic staff.

After all these horrors, they come to the Bowre, a place of apparent peace and rest after toil:

> A place pickt out by choice of best aliue,
> That natures worke by art can imitate:
> In which what euer in this worldly state
> Is sweet, and pleasing vnto liuing sense,
> Or that may dayntiest fantasie aggrate,
> Was poured forth with plentifull dispence,
> And made there to abound with lauish affluence.
>
> (II.xii.42)

Here they must face even more pernicious dangers: falsified nature, carved ivory, a goodly welcome. Even song tempts them away from their quest: they must, that is, learn to overcome even the pleasures of art. Guyon almost succumbs to sexual pleasure, but the Palmer pulls him away from the lovely naked maidens in the fountain and on to his final, almost horrifyingly destructive act.

Spenser's method, as we saw in our consideration of Book I, is to allow the reader to learn by experiencing the very temptations his heroes must face. He uses that same technique here, but in a rather different way. In Book I the hero encounters many temptations along the way, learning with each to reject them, to recognize the presence of evil disguised as good. By the end of the book, the reader, like the Redcrosse Knight, should be thoroughly enough schooled in the ways of holiness to recognize its enemies and overcome or avoid them. The evil of the dragon in canto xi of Book I is unequivocal, and no reader would mistake the knight's animosity toward it for inappropriate behavior. The same cannot be said for Guyon's climactic adventure at the end of Book II, the violent, almost frenzied, destruction of the Bowre of Bliss.

Readers of Spenser today and even for the past three centuries or more are for the most part conservators of art—those with special (often antiquarian) interests in literature and in art. It is only natural that they should find the apparent attack on the artful Bowre in this final canto distasteful and should either seek almost desperately for a rationale or condemn Guyon as a thoughtless prig. But in fact, in Book II, as in Book I, Spenser is tempting us to sin, and in the Bowre episode he demonstrates just how powerful that temptation can be. If we find this artificial garden too beautiful, if we are seduced by its charms, then we are likely to fall victim to art's evil side. Spenser, like his contemporaries, recognized that misuse of any art can lead to evil. Acrasia has built a place of beauty, but it is a false beauty, like Duessa's or Lucifera's, used to disguise the true evil lurking within. Only if it is destroyed can the weaker sort, the Grylls of the world, be protected from it. In this book we learn that temperance is a matter of overcoming not only that which is ugly, but also that which is beautiful as well. We must reject a life devoted exclusively to Mammon, but we must avoid also the temptations of a life devoted exclusively to idle art. If we cannot do both, then we, unlike Sir Guyon, have no hope of achieving true temperance.

7

Book III:
The Legend of Chastity

If Spenser retained his original masterplan in constructing Books I and II, by the time he got to Book III, that plan had obviously changed considerably. The first two books of *The Faerie Queene* are often considered together, if not as a unit, at least as a matching set, and many readers who have read both are convinced they have fully sampled all Spenser has to offer. Such readers approach Book III expecting the same sort of structure—the exploits of a single hero or a hero and his companion, events progressing chronologically throughout the book, with the narrative clearly laid out and easily followed. When they enter the world of Book III, these readers are always surprised and occasionally disappointed, but more often delighted with the variety Spenser presents in his poem. To better understand that variety, let us examine first some of the major differences between Book III and Books I and II, not the least of which is that the hero of this book is a woman.

While Books I and II concentrate essentially on the exploits of their single heroes, Book III has a different focus. In I and II we almost constantly focus on Redcrosse (and Una) or Guyon; in nearly all instances, they are in the "foreground" of the action. In Book III, however, while Britomart is the foreground character, we focus on the events that are in the background. Britomart serves as a link through a series of "tableaux." Redcrosse and Guyon *act,* and we focus upon their *actions;* Britomart *travels,* and we focus upon the events she leads us to.

Book I is a straightforward narrative in that there are just two main characters and we focus on one or the other of them in every canto, shifting from one to the other in a predictable fashion. Our focus, furthermore, is nearly always on the allegorical significance of the Redcrosse Knight's challenge of and search for Holiness in the form of Una. We either focus on the quest or on the object of the quest. Book II is, if anything, even more straightforward. Guyon appears in every canto except iii (where we see his antithesis, Braggadochio, using Guyon's horse and lance) and xi (where Arthur defends the House of Alma from its enemies).

In Book III, however, the narrative is hardly straightforward in virtually any sense. First, the titular hero, Britomart, appears in only seven of the cantos; she has no direct role in cantos v, vi, vii, or viii—a long stretch without her—and only a minor part in canto ix, then again does not appear at all in canto x. For fully half of the Book, we do not focus on her. Furthermore, cantos ii and iii are in large part concerned with a flashback, a retrospective narrative in which we learn of Britomart's past. Only in cantos i, iv, xi, and xii, then, do we actually focus on Britomart's actions in the present.

In addition, unlike Books I and II, Book III is not complete in itself; not only do we have an inordinate number of characters stepping in from earlier books (Arthur, Timias, Guyon, Redcrosse, Belphoebe, Braggadochio, Sir Satyrane, the Satyrs), but many of the main adventures of III must wait until Book IV to reach fruition—including Britomart's first meeting with Artegall, the object of her quest. Book III (The Legend of Chastity) must, in short, depend upon Book IV (The Legend of Friendship), as success in marriage must depend on both friendship and chastity.

As Spenser progressed from Book I through Book IV, he in effect broadened his scope. Some—Thomas P. Roche, Jr. predominant among them—argue that Books III and IV best represent Spenser's stated hope to "overgo Ariosto," for in these books of *The Faerie Queene* Spenser most nearly approaches what we find in the Italian chivalric romances—and in them Spenser approximates many of Ariosto's scenes and characters.

While this assessment is patently true, there is also a sense of Spenser's growing powers as a narrative poet, his ability to tell a good tale in the manner of the Ariostan romance he so clearly admired. Spenser is continuing his development as a literary artist. *The Shepheardes Calender* is, in the strictest view, a series of discrete narrative poems, "short stories" as it were, although a collection that, like James Joyce's *Dubliners,* has some unifying threads running throughout. The first two books of *The Faerie Queene* are akin to more complex, longer stories. (Book I, for example, is almost precisely twice as long as the whole of *The Shepheardes Calender.*) In Books III and IV, we see Spenser stretching toward an even longer continuous narrative. If *The Shepheardes Calender* is Spenser's *Dubliners,* then perhaps we could say that Book I or II represents his *Portrait of the Artist as a Young Man* (or, more aptly, the first version of that book, *Stephen Hero*), and Books III and IV his *Ulysses*. This metaphor should not, however, be carried too far. That Books III and IV are tightly linked is widely recognized, but Spenser is not in any way the "Father of the Modern Novel," or even its spiritual godfather.[25] The point, however, is valid: the narrative mode changes, becomes rather more complex and, for some readers who feel their expectations have been violated, less satisfying. The problem is certainly not solved for these readers when we return, in Book V, to the more familiar allegorical world, as we shall see. Regardless of the reason for it, the result of the structural shift is that Book III initially seems far less organized, less complete. But that impression is quite incorrect. The structure of this book differs from that of Books I and II, but the plan for the book is no less coherent.

While Prince Arthur appears in Book III, his role here also deviates significantly from the part he plays in Books I and II. In those books, he intervenes to rescue the hero—Redcrosse from Orgoglio's dungeon, Guyon from his unprotected swoon. Here, however, he has no direct effect upon Britomart's adventures, a significant departure from the apparent master plan of the earlier books. Furthermore, he enters this book in the very first stanza, rather than delaying his entry until a crucial point of the narrative so he can rescue the hero, as he did in Books I and II. To understand why Spenser has allowed these departures, we need to look at Britomart's past and the beginning of her quest.

The narrative shifts to the past in cantos ii and iii for the account of how Britomart saw an image of Artegall in her father's mirror, fell in love with his image, and was taken to Merlin for advice by Glauce, her nurse. In these cantos we are reminded of Arthur's account of his own past and, particularly, his dream-encounter with Gloriana, the Faerie Queene, in Book I. There we are told that Arthur, like Britomart, learned something of his heritage from Merlin:

> Thither the great Magicien *Merlin* came,
>> As was his vse, ofttimes to visit me:
>> For he had charge my discipline to frame,
>> And Tutours nouriture to ouersee.
>> Him oft and oft I askt in priuitie,
>> Of what loines and what lignage I did spring:
>> Whose aunswere bad me still assured bee,
>> That I was sonne and heire vnto a king,
> As time in her iust terme the truth to light should bring.
>
> (I.ix.5)

By telling Britomart of her future with Artegall and the story of their progeny, Merlin indirectly serves as the impetus for her adventures in search of her future husband. Similarly, Arthur believes that Merlin may have been the impetus for his journey to and throughout Faerie Land:

> For whither he through fatall deepe foresight
>> Me hither sent, for cause to me vnghest,

> Or that fresh bleeding wound, which day and night
> Whilome doth rancle in my riuen brest,
> With forced fury following his behest,
> Me hither brought by wayes yet neuer found,
> You to haue helpt I hold my selfe yet blest.
>
> (I.ix.7)

Arthur sets out in search of his past, his parentage, which in turn will lead him to his future. Britomart, more directly, sets out in search of her future. But they are linked not only by the quest, but also because Merlin provides the impetus for their searches.

Furthermore, Arthur's adventures lead him to the Chamber of Memory in Book II where, as we have seen, he is given the opportunity to read of the history of Briton, to see his nation's future in some detail. When Britomart visits Merlin, she is given a similar opportunity, but only to see her own (and her progeny's) future. Both Arthur and Britomart are given a history of Britain—Arthur from the beginnings to his own day, Britomart from her time into the future—to the glories of the Tudors, Spenser's own monarchs. (The linking portion of this history of Britain—the period from the coming of Arthur to the coming of Britomart—is related in canto ix, the story of Troy and Troynovant told by Paridell in Malbecco's castle.)

These similarities suggest that Britomart is the female counterpart of Arthur, born of royalty and progenitor of a great nation (and thus often a metaphorical representation of Queen Elizabeth). And this, of course, explains why Arthur does not play the same crucial roles in Book III that he does in Books I and II: he is not needed to rescue the hero because Britomart is already there.

Britomart's quest resembles Arthur's in that both seek for a loved one, and in both instances that love-object has appeared in a vision. The visions, however, are quite different, and in their differences they indicate a crucial distinction between the quests. Arthur is not certain whether he has actually seen Gloriana or merely dreamed of her:

> Most goodly glee and louely blandishment
> She to me made, and bad me loue her deare,
> For dearely sure her loue was to me bent,

As when iust time expired should appeare.
But whether dreams delude, or true it were,
Was neuer hart so rauisht with delight,
Ne liuing man like words did euer heare,
As she to me deliuered all that night;
And at her parting said, She Queene of Faeries hight.

(I.ix.14)

Whether vision or reality, Gloriana came to Arthur, and both, apparently, know of it. Britomart, on the other hand, sees only the image of Artegall in her father's mirror. Looking for herself, her own image, in the mirror, she sees instead the image of the man with whom destiny has linked her. Artegall knows nothing of her vision, but the nature of the image, the linking of the self and the other indicates that Britomart and Artegall are to be not just married, but incomplete without each other. Britomart, in effect, must find Artegall in order to find herself.

This search for the self in another fits with the concept of chastity that governs this book. Chastity as Spenser perceived it is difficult to define, for it involves more than mere virginity, abstinence from sexual contact. Rather, it extends into the sexuality of married life, where it encompasses marital fidelity and loyalty to one's self as well as one's spouse. So that we can better understand the concept of chastity, Spenser provides us with a broad range of examples, both negative and positive, through deficiency and through excess. For deficiency, he shows us Malecasta, Hellenore, Argante, and the Snowy Florimell. Three forms of excess are demonstrated in Florimell, Belphoebe, and Amoret, two of whom are capable of reaching true married chastity, while the third, Belphoebe, has elected to remain both chaste and unmarried.

Britomart encounters the first demonstration of a lack of chastity when she separates from Arthur, Timias, and Guyon in canto i and travels to Castle Joyous, the castle of Malecasta, a representative of the chivalric or courtly love ideal. Malecasta surrounds herself with knights who challenge passersby in her name, defeating them and thus increasing her retinue. The Redcrosse Knight has been so challenged and is attempting to defend the beauty of his own lady, Una, against

69

six challengers when Britomart arrives. Her rescue of Redcrosse and subsequent adventure in Castle Joyous is meant to demonstrate the power of her chastity and the evils of courtly love.

Malecasta represents the courtly love tradition carried to its extreme, not being content with a single knight to idolize her, but wanting all who pass to fall into her power. Britomart handily defeats her six knights and resists her advances, although she is lightly wounded by an arrow shot by Gardante ("watching"), perhaps an indication that the mere sight of the sumptuousness of Malecasta's castle has some appeal to her, certainly an indication that she has been rather careless in protecting her own chastity and must learn to be more wary.

The second major example we see of behavior reflecting a deficiency of chastity occurs in canto vii, where we meet the Squire of Dames and Argante—male and female sexual excess. The Squire of Dames, who has a "louly face, made fit for to deceiue / Fraile Ladies hart with loues consuming rage" (III.vii.46), claims some 300 sexual conquests. He offers as his excuse for such excess that he has acted at the behest of the woman he loves, who has also forced him to seek out an equal number of truly chaste women. But he has found only one, "a Damzell of low degree" (III.7.59). Aside from her, he says, he has discovered no other "that chastity did for itself embrace."

> Argante is a fit companion for the Squire, for she
>> Did wallow in all . . . fleshly myre,
>> And sufferd beasts her body to deflowre:
>> So whot she burned in that lustfull fyre,
> Yet all that might not slake her sensuall desyre.
>
> But ouer all the countrey she did raunge,
>> To seeke young men, to quench her flaming thrust,
> And feed her fancy with delightfull chaunge.
>>>> (III.vii.49–50)

The Squire and Argante represent the ultimate degeneration of sexuality, unchastity in the extremes of satyriasis and nymphomania. They are certainly not forms of unchaste behavior Britomart is likely to emulate, nor do we really need to be told to avoid their behavior. In fact, the Squire of Dames's tale seems to be taken largely from a similar cynical episode in Ariosto's *Orlando Furioso* (Book 28), a tale in which two men search the world over for a woman who can remain true to two lovers. Here, though, Spenser has more than merely prurient or cynical motives, for with these characters he helps define chastity by showing us its precise opposite.

In the following episode, we meet the Snowy Florimell, who, like Malecasta, parodies a literary tradition. Made by the witch for her loutish son after the real Florimell departs, even this false Florimell can arouse lust (and inspire good actions) from the various characters she encounters. In her flawless beauty she resembles the "perfect woman" described in Petrarchan love sonnets; in fact, her manufacture is described in terms of Petrarchan clichés:

> The substance, whereof she the bodie made,
> >   Was purest snow in massie mould congeald,
> >   Which she had gathered in a shadie glade
> >   Of the Riphaean hils, to her reueald
> >   By errant Sprights, but from all men conceald:
> >   The same she tempred with fine Mercury,
> >   And virgin wex, that neuer yet was seald,
> >   And mingled them with perfect vermily,
> > That like a liuely sanguine it seem'd to the eye.
>
> In stead of eyes two burning lampes she set
> >   In siluer sockets, shyning like the skyes,
> >   And a quicke mouing Spirit did arret
> >   To stirre and roll them, like a womans eyes;
> >   In stead of yellow lockes she did diuise,
> >   With golden wyre to weaue her curled head;
> >   Yet golden wyre was not so yellow thrise
> >   As Florimells faire haire: and in the stead
> > Of life, she put a Spright to rule the carkasse dead.
> >   (III.viii.6—7)

71

As these stanzas should make clear, Spenser does not neglect the potential comedy of this situation: his Snowy Florimell is a parody of the perfect Petrarchan woman, and it is fitting that the first person to challenge the witch's son for his new toy is a parody of knighthood—Braggadochio—who promptly loses her to another challenger without a fight. Later, as we shall see in our consideration of the tournament celebrating the marriage of Marinell and Florimell in Book V, Spenser will make even some of his more serious knights look foolish over the Snowy Florimell.

While the episode at Malecasta's Castle Joyous represents unchaste behavior in the courtly love tradition, the Hellenore/Malbecco/Paridell episode of cantos ix and x shows us the effects of adultery or unchaste behavior in marriage. This episode represents degenerate sexuality, both marital and extra-marital, abstemious and excessive. It is as much a parody of chastity as Braggadochio is a parody of knightly honor in Book II. Malbecco's castle is a home in which chastity is destroyed, perhaps even its possibility denied, by his entirely foolish attitudes toward his wife, by Paridell's seducing and deserting Hellenore, by Hellenore's turning into a mere sex object for the Satyrs, an emblem for perverted sexuality, and finally by Malbecco's turning into an owl-like beast, the very emblem of jealousy.

Furthermore, in the recounting—and replaying—of the kidnapping and seduction of Helen of Troy, we see the potential effects of unchaste behavior on the body politic, much the same as we see the effects of intemperance of a different sort in the Briton Chronicles of Book II, canto x. The story of Troy in this section is the middle portion of the history of Britain, fitting between Arthur's reading in the Chamber of Memory (II.x) and Britomart's hearing of her progeny from Merlin (III.iii). With this section, then, we have been given a complete history of Britain from its beginnings to the present day.

This entire episode, encompassing cantos ix and x, parallels the same cantos in Book I (Redcrosse's admission to and cure in the House of Holiness and his vision of the New Jerusalem) and in Book II (Arthur's and Guyon's learning of the wonders of the human body and brain in the Castle of Alma and their reading of the histories of their respective nations in the Chamber of Memory) in that, like the ninth and tenth cantos of the earlier books, this passage may be considered the allegorical center of the book, even though the episode does not focus directly on the titular heroine of that book. Here we not only learn the final, linking portion of the history of Britain, but we see (after Britomart has left, interestingly enough) the disastrous effects of the failure of chastity. We learn, unequivocally, that mere marriage is insufficient to ensure or protect chastity. We could argue that this is a lesson Britomart must learn if she is to find complete success in her marriage to Artegall—but Spenser, I suspect, would insist that we need this lesson far more than his heroine—and thus she may leave before it is acted out.

So far we have examined what chastity is not, but definition by negation is always insufficient; Spenser also shows us examples of what chastity can be by demonstrating its various faces in the persons of Florimell, Belphoebe, and Amoret. Looking at these three and Britomart, we can better understand chastity in its most nearly perfect form. While Britomart may be perfectly controlled, Florimell is her precise opposite, representing chastity that is under constant assault, always at the will of others. She remains chaste only out of the good offices of others and her own swiftness of foot. Britomart, on the other hand, remains chaste entirely of her own volition, through her own martial powers. Britomart represents, one could say, Chastity Militant, with a single driving force, her desire to discover Artegall, whom she has seen only in a vision in her mirror, while Florimell is chastity in flight. Florimell flees from dangers that are both imagined and real; Britomart pursues a love that is both imagined and real.

Florimell's first appearance in the book is in flight, when she rushes onto the scene in canto i, pursued by the Forester. Timias chases her attacker, while Arthur and Guyon set out in pursuit of the fleeing victim. She does not realize that her danger is past and, as she will do throughout the book, runs from a lesser to a greater danger, away from rescue in the hope of saving herself through mere flight. Chastity is an active, not a passive virtue, and we are meant to see in Florimell that flight from its threats is not in itself sufficient, for running from the enemies of chastity will lead us always into the path of other, still more powerful foes.

We are reminded of Florimell's fleeing again in cantos iv and v, when Arthur continues his search for her, but we do not focus directly on her again until canto vii, when she comes to the home of the witch and, expecting succor, finds instead the witch's retarded but nonetheless libidinous son. Sneaking away from this potentially threatening (but not immediately dangerous) situation, she is pursued by the witch's beast, and in fleeing from personified Lust, she falls prey to other lustful creatures. She seeks rescue from a kindly fisherman—who proves to be far less kindly in canto viii, once he has her alone on his boat. She is rescued from the lecherous fisherman by the seagod Proteus, who, in turn, has his own designs on her. And that is the last we see of Florimell until Book IV.

There is in her adventures a progression of dangers she must face, some quite real, others imagined. She moves from relatively public danger to greater and greater isolation—and hence more and more serious threats. The Forester's threat was real enough, but occurring as it did in the well-traveled area of the forest, chances of rescue were fairly significant. She flees to the witch's home, though, where in the society of a single family, she is less subject to rescue and must, once more, flee to nature, where she can be both pursued by lust and rescued by Sir Satyrane. Her next encounter occurs in isolation with her attacker aboard his boat, then in the absolute isolation of the sea, where her attacker rules supreme. There is, in addition, another progression in this episode, for the witch's son, though human in form, resembles Shakespeare's Caliban in his degeneracy, while the beast loosed by the witch seems to be a step above the son in both its power and ambition—at least it is able to act on its own. It is, however, stopped at the water's edge where Florimell joins company with a fisherman who, while a fully rational person, lets the water control his boat, and she is rescued from his lust by Proteus, who controls the waters and even his own shape—but not his own desires. We have, in other words, lust at several levels: base or subhuman, bestial, human, and godly, all threatening Florimell's fearful chastity.

Flight from threats to chastity need not always be caused by one's own fear, though, as we see with Marinell, the object of Florimell's unrequited love. Marinell's mother, Cymoent, having been told that he will be killed by a woman, has forced him to avoid the company of women. The one man Florimell loves is the only man who will not pursue her. In spite of his attempts to avoid women, Marinell is defeated by Britomart, thus both fulfilling his mother's fears and making a mockery of them. In attempting to avoid all female companionship, Marinell fails to realize that a woman might be wearing knightly armor and thus chooses an opponent unwisely. The attempt to keep him removed from women has only resulted in his vulnerability, an irony Spenser makes clear: "His mother bad him womens loue to hate, / For she of womans force did feare no harme" (III.iv.27). Chastity that results only from external forces is clearly as insufficient as chastity that results from mere fear.

While Florimell and Marinell maintain their chastity out of fear, another chaste character, Belphoebe, maintains hers out of conviction. Belphoebe, twin sister of Amoret, was raised by Diana as a devotee of the chaste life. She is, of course, content with her convictions, but unfortunately Timias, infatuated with her, is not. His reaction to their situation illustrates another possible result of misunderstood chastity: the pain of unrequited love. Those pains come to Timias when, whether because of his weakened physical condition or his emotional and moral immaturity, he fails to see that the platonic relationship Belphoebe offers him is of a higher order than mere sexual desire.

Belphoebe is unthreatened by passion, in absolutely no danger of losing her chastity because she is totally in control both of herself and of the others she faces. She already shows us this quality in Book II when she is attacked by impotently lustful Braggadochio. She does not engage him in battle, but merely leaves, a prudent thing to do and thus emblematic of the concerns of Book II. In her relationship with Timias, she is similarly in charge: she doctors the wounded Timias and thus controls him completely—and never seems to realize that he has fallen in love with her, such is her innocence of emotional matters. At the same time, however, as we shall see in Book IV, she experiences either jealousy or some other sort of uncontrolled emotion when she discovers the wounded Amoret in Timias's arms: "Is this the faith?" she cries out, and storms away, perhaps simply jealous or, more in keeping with her character, disappointed that Timias cannot be as pure and chaste as she. Belphoebe is a careful and patient nurse to Timias's physical wounds, but her own convictions prevent her from seeing his desires and thus the true cause of his illness. She is so free of lust herself that she seems incapable of recognizing it in others, even when she is its cause.

The account of the birth and rearing of Belphoebe and her twin sister, Amoret, occupies the central sixth canto of Book III. Born of Chrysogone in a miraculous virgin birth (they are fathered by the rays of the sun), the daughters are taken from their mother as she sleeps, even through their delivery: "She bore withouten paine, that she conceiued / Withouten pleasure" (III.v.27). Belphoebe is taken to Diana for her training, Amoret to Venus.

Venus's Garden of Adonis in Book III, where Amoret is reared, is the counterpart to Acrasia's Bowre of Bliss in Book II, and it is not coincidental that the mistress of the garden in Book III is represented as loving, wholesome, productive, while that of Book II is merely lustful. Acrasia's garden is artificial, unproductive, even destructive; the Garden of Adonis is natural, fecund, productive, an eternal garden where even Adonis lives and where all life finds in its circular pattern of decay and renewal the "eterne in mutabilitie" (III.vi.47) that Spenser will find so comforting in the Cantos of Mutabilitie.

Even with her idyllic childhood and education, however, Amoret is not fully prepared for the ways of the world. She goes to Gloriana's court and falls in love with and marries Scudamour, but she is taken captive at their wedding feast by the horrid Busyrane, who keeps her from her husband, feeding on her fears of wedded life, fears both of her own sexuality and of consummating the life for which she was reared. She cannot be rescued by Scudamour, even though he knows full well where she is, because he is in fact the cause of her captivity, the source of her fears. Only Britomart, another woman and the very figure of chastity, can release her from Busyrane's imprisonment. But before she can reach Amoret, Britomart must pass through the wall of fire and experience the Mask of Cupid. As Thomas Roche has pointed out, the figures of this mask are "dramatic presentations of common sonnet metaphors."[26] This should not surprise us, for we have already seen Spenser using such metaphors to describe the components of which the Snowy Florimell is made.

With her rescue of Amoret, Britomart is significantly closer to being prepared to meet Artegall; she now has a far more sophisticated, mature view of love than she had on first seeing Artegall's image in her father's mirror. She has gone from being a mere girl, turning for comfort to her nurse, at the beginning of her quest, to a mature woman at the end of the book. In Britomart we are to see a complex mean, not between two extremes, but among three, as if we must reach into a third dimension to place her accurately on a scale where she can actually be between (and not just among) Belphoebe, Florimell, and Amoret. She is neither so militantly chaste as to be self-canceling like Belphoebe, nor so terrified of love as to be helpless on her own, threatened by everyone she meets, as Florimell is. Nor is she, finally, so single-mindedly devoted to one way of life that she is afraid of the final commitment to it, as Amoret is. Finding the balance has perhaps been more her goal in this book than finding Artegall, for not until she achieves that balance is she prepared to continue her quest. Not only chaste, she now understands the nature of chastity in married love.

8

Book IV:
The Legend of Friendship

Readers who are troubled by Spenser's departure in Book III from the modes established by Books I and II are generally more disturbed by the presentation of friendship in Book IV. In this book Spenser departs even more radically from the apparent plan of the first two books, the single knight on a single, unified adventure.

While Britomart's appearances in Book III are relatively sporadic, there is still simply no doubt that she is the hero of that book, if not always the focus of our attention. The same certainly cannot be said of Cambell and Triamond (or Telamond),[27] the titular heroes of Book IV; not only do they have a relatively late first appearance, well into the second canto, but they are the central object of our focus only in the latter part of canto ii and in canto iii, where their story is told retrospectively. In canto iv they appear as the victors in the second day of the Tournament of Maidenhead, and then they effectively disappear from the remainder of the book. The titular heroes, in other words, serve only minor, perhaps emblematic functions and are subordinate to the dominant role of Britomart and her search for Artegall, Scudamour, and Amoret—even Florimell and Marinell. In fact, as canto iii makes clear, Cambell and Triamond's real story is completed before we even meet them. They have dispatched their enmity and, through the magical intervention of Cambina, become fast and undying friends.

Cambell and Triamond can accurately be said to be more symbols or emblems of Book IV's concerns than heroes of the Book. This primary difference between Book IV and the earlier books has created problems for readers who come to it expecting this book to parallel in technique the earlier parts of *The Faerie Queene*. Despite the obvious differences, however, Spenser does continue the basic mode of the earlier parts of the poem, for in Book IV, as in the earlier books, he continues to demonstrate the intended virtue to the reader by using his text to draw the reader into a better understanding of that virtue through experiencing it.

It seems clear that Spenser found his original plan—a single hero for each book—to be unsatisfactory for this book dealing with the first of three public or community virtues. Friendship, unlike holiness, temperance, and chastity, cannot be achieved alone. In fact, the very movement of the entire *Faerie Queene* has been to this point (and will continue to be in Books V and VI) from the internal toward increasingly external virtues. Holiness, the virtue of Book I, is an entirely internal virtue; the holy person may venture into the outside world, as the Redcrosse Knight does in his adventures in Faery Land, but the virtue is, by its very nature, fully internal and internalized. Holiness involves the self and that self's attitudes toward a supreme being; it is not concerned directly with others.

Temperance moves internal virtues toward the world outside the self. It requires an internalization of values, but it is manifested in how one adapts that internalization to an attitude toward the external world. In its essence, temperance could perhaps be called a tolerance toward others, which results from earned self-confidence. Chastity turns still more outward, for it is concerned primarily (although not exclusively) with what we might call attitudinal sexuality, that is, with one's attitude toward and engagement in sexuality and closely related issues—desire, lust, love.

Friendship, finally, requires a broader social view. One may be holy, temperate, chaste entirely on one's own, but to be one's own best friend is to miss entirely the point about friendship and degenerate into narcissism. Holiness, Temperance, and Chastity may exist in society and permit the presence of others, but friendship can exist *only* in society and requires the presence of an other.

In the second part of *The Faerie Queene,* then, we turn our attention to external, public, community virtues, those which have to do with our fledgling knight's behavior not just as a holy, temperate, and chaste individual, but also as an active, engaged member of society. And, as we shall see, the externalization increases from friendship, the relationship of the individual to other specific individuals, through justice, the relationship of the individual to the codified rules of behavior in society, to courtesy, the relationship of the individual to the inherent, uncodified, unstated expectations of social behavior. We move, that is, from the individual's relationship with God (Holiness), to the self (Temperance), to a significant and specified other (Chastity, particularly married chastity), to a broader range of others (Friendship), to the structures of society (Justice, particularly law and equity), and, finally, to the very basis of human society (Courtesy). Furthermore, as Roche has pointed out, the first six books of *The Faerie Queene* are like a diptych: chastity is the private virtue of which friendship is the public counterpart; temperance (private) corresponds to justice (public); and holiness (private) corresponds to courtesy (public).[28] The relationship among the virtues in the six books, in other words, is more than just a progression; it is a unifying device as well.

Book IV, like the entire poem, is also united in metaphorical ways. Given the nature of friendship, it is not coincidental that we see together in this book so many of the characters we met earlier. As we have seen in Books II and III, part of Spenser's method is to have characters from the previous book appear early, thus linking both the narratives and the virtues. In Book IV he follows his method with a vengeance. Canto i opens with Britomart and Amoret continuing their adventures from the ending of Book III. We soon encounter Duessa (from Books I and II), Paridell (from III.viii), Scudamour (from III.xi), and Glauce, who was separated from Britomart in Book III. In canto ii we find the Snowy Florimell and Sir Ferraugh, the knight to whom Braggadochio surrendered her in III.viii, and the Squire of Dames, who appears first in III.vii. In canto iv we encounter Braggadochio, who first appeared stealing Guyon's horse and debating Belphoebe in II.iii, and Sir Satyrane, who rescues Una from the Satyrs in I.vi. We do not see the heroes of Books I and II, but with the appearances of Duessa, Redcrosse's primary rival, and Braggadochio, Guyon's foil, we are certainly reminded of them.

In canto vi we finally meet Artegall, whose appearance we have been awaiting since we learned of Britomart's vision of him in her mirror in canto ii of Book III. Furthermore, Spenser has been carefully preparing us for the moment they meet, not only in Britomart's quest but in the several times she reveals herself to others as a woman. The moment at which Artegall discovers that his opponent is a woman is quite striking. A stroke of his sword knocks her helmet loose:

> With that her angels face, vnseene afore,
> Like to the ruddie morne appeard in sight,
> Deawed with siluer drops, through sweating sore,
> But somewhat redeer, then beseem's aright,
> Through toylesome heate and labour of her weary fight.
>
> And round about the same, her yellow heare
> Hauing through stirring loosd their wonted band,
> Like to a golden border did appeare,
> Framed in goldsmithes forge with cunning hand.
>
> (IV.vi.19–20)

With the description of her hair in particular we are taken back to the first canto of this book, when Britomart reveals her gender, much to the surprise of her opponents and delight of Amoret:

> With that her glistering helmet she vnlaced;
> Which doft, her golden lockes, that were vp bound
> Still in a knot, vnto her heeles downe traced,
> And like a silken veile in compasse round
> About her backe and all her bodie wound.
>
> (IV.i.13)

We have, in fact, been prepared for this moment since the first canto of Book III, when Britomart rejects Malecasta's advances in Castle Joyous and is revealed to Malecasta's champions and the Redcrosse Knight "all in her snow-white smocke, with locks vnbownd" (III.i.63). The event we have anticipated not just throughout Britomart's fight with Artegall, but since the very beginning of Book III at last comes to fruition in this book.

Having seen Britomart and Artegall at last united, we see Timias and Belphoebe again in canto vii; our last direct contact with them was in III.v. Prince Arthur makes his first appearance in this book in the same canto. Finally, in canto xii we see Marinell, whom we saw first in III.iv, where he is wounded by Britomart, and Cymoent, who takes him home to be cured. We also see Proteus again and his captive, Florimell, whom we first encountered in III.i, when she becomes the occasion for so many of the episodic adventures of that book. Florimell, then, frames Books III and IV, first rushing through the forest of III.i, setting characters off in separate directions to rescue her, then marrying her beloved Marinell at the beginning of Book V. The trail she established in III.i stretches its way through 25 cantos, a record for *The Faerie Queene*.

But Florimell and Marinell are not the only characters united in Book IV. Here, Britomart finally meets and is betrothed to the object of her quest, Artegall, in canto vi. Scudamour and Amoret are, presumably, reunited, and we learn of their first meeting when Scudamour narrates his tale of how he claimed Amoret from the Temple of Venus only to lose her on their wedding day. Timias and Belphoebe, united in a patient-nurse relationship in Book III, become separated in IV.vi when Belphoebe discovers that Timias's nursing methods with the wounded Amoret are closer to what he expected of her than what she offered to him. But they, too, are reconciled in IV.vii, although Belphoebe must perforce retain her virginal nature.

And finally even Braggadochio and the Snowy Florimell, separated by the former's cowardice in III.viii are back together again, a couple fully deserving of each other, in canto v, when the Snowy Florimell, true to her own nature, selects the one false knight from among the assembled warriors—much to the amusing dismay of the others. As Rosemary Freeman points out, Book III is a book of separation, IV a book of reconciliation.[29]

In this book of reunited friends, though, it is ironic that Timias must wait until Book VI to be reunited with Prince Arthur. They meet, but in his despair over losing Belphoebe Timias is so disheveled that even Arthur does not recognize him. Arriving at Timias's cabin, expecting to find "some holy Hermit," Arthur finds instead

> this wretched man,
> Spending his daies in dolour and despaire,
> And through long fasting woxen pale and wan,
> All ouergrowen with rude and rugged haire;
> That albeit his owne deare Squire he were,
> Yet he him knew not, ne auiz'd at all,
> But like strange wight, whom he had seene no where,
> Saluting him, gan into speach to fall,
> And pitty much his plight, that liu'd like outcast thrall.
>
> (IV.vii.43)

Timias, aided by innocent nature in the form of the bird, is reunited with Belphoebe, but he is not yet ready to be reunited with Arthur in this book. Arthur, however, nonetheless plays a major role in helping to reunite others. He helps Aemylia and Amoret escape from the Cave of Lust, restoring Aemylia to Amyas, and kills Corflambo, thus saving Placidas, who can in turn be reunited with his friend Amyas and married to Poeana. We may also presume that he has reunited Amoret and Scudamour—although Spenser does not specify that they are reunited in this book as he had in the original ending of Book III in the 1590 edition. Spenser may simply have neglected to insert the stanzas in which Scudamour and Amoret are reunited; they would certainly fit at the end of canto ix (following stanza 39). On the other hand, he also may have intentionally left that reunion out, indicating that while Scudamour has sought valiantly for his wife, and she fled fearfully danger after danger, there is still no reason to believe that she is any more to him than the prize she represents in his account of winning her.

There is more to Book IV than just reconciliation, though, for as we have noted before, Spenser's method of teaching his "gentleman or noble person" is to have the reader experience the virtue in question. This goal is achieved in this book partly through showing us various exempla of friendship, emblems or personified abstractions, or even more nearly "rounded" characters (Britomart in particular). But he also achieves the goal through the very structure of the Book. As Freeman has observed, one of the striking features of Book IV is that episodes in the early cantos do not coincide with the beginnings and ends of cantos as they do in earlier books.[30] That is, an episode ends at midcanto and another begins there. Canto v, for example, begins with the Tournament of Maidenhead and the comic award of Flori-mell's girdle to the Snowy Florimell, then shifts to Scudamour and Glauce as they arrive at the House of Care; canto vi opens by continuing Scudamour's search for Amoret. Amoret disappears at the end of canto vi, but our attention is turned to her at the opening of vii. Canto vii then finishes with Timias, rejected by Belphoebe, becoming a hermit. In canto viii Timias and Belphoebe are reunited, but by the end of the canto our attention is on Placidas and Amyas, whom we will follow into the next canto.

Spenser is trying to illustrate the unifying nature of friendship by using this structural device—making his book an emblem of itself. This is the book of friendship, a virtue of unity rather than individuality, and the very unity of the book is achieved by the book itself rather than by its individual cantos. Cantos are linked to form complete episodes just as friends are linked to form complete social units. This analogy should not be carried too far, of course, but nonetheless Book IV does not have a particular hero because the virtue it represents does not call for a single hero and such a hero is not necessary for thematic unity. The book is in itself a unifying force, a self-reflexive, self-referen-tial allegory. It represents unity in diversity, just as friendship is a unifying device for seemingly diverse people.

The Legend of Friendship

The same can be said for one of the great moments of Book IV, the Marriage of the Thames and the Medway in canto xi, the allegorical center of this book, representing the uniting forces of both friendship and marriage. Spenser is portraying a mythological joining of the rivers, but a real confluence as well, one in which the Thames and the Medway, two distinct rivers, come together to form a single river, which still bears both their waters, but intermingled in such a way as to be indistinguishable.

The confluence of the rivers is a metaphor for this book. Just as we cannot tell merely by glancing at the canto openings or endings where one episode begins and another ends, we cannot distinguish that precise point at which the Thames and the Medway become one. More important, just as we cannot tell one river from the other in a confluence, the other characters cannot tell Cambell from Triamond at the Tournament of Dames when they wear each other's armor and give each other credit, nor can we, for that matter, really tell Triamond from his brothers Priamond and Diamond, whose souls fled to him when they were defeated. Friendship, love, indeed this book, are all confluences. It is for this reason, then, that Britomart, the Knight of Chastity, must wait until this book of friendship to meet her beloved Artegall. One can conceive of a Book III in which they meet and marry, but marriage without friendship, even marriage based upon true and absolute married chastity—that is, devotion and honesty—is insufficient for completion of the marriage partners. Without friendship, marriage is mere sexual union, a biological, but not a social unit.

But friendship must, of course, also be distinguished from other relationships that, to a casual observer, may appear to be the same. In particular, friendship, which is a kind of concord, must be distinguished from alliance or even mere proximity, and Spenser gives examples of these relationships so we can better recognize them when we encounter them in life. Friendship can easily be confused with alliance; alliance results from common, though temporary, goals, and when those goals are met (or fail to be met), alliances fail. Those not based on friendship easily become enmity. The temporary alliances at the Tournament of Maidenhead illustrate this principle, for many of the knights on each side have nothing in common but a temporary alliance against the other side, an alliance of convenience, which will dissolve when the occasion for its formation has ceased to be. And many of those same allies will soon become enemies once more.

What quickly becomes apparent at the Tournament is that we cannot call one side "good," the other "bad." There are characters with whom we are meant to sympathize on both sides as well as those whom we are meant to disdain. The sides formed are not intended to demonstrate anything more than temporary alliances—and it is significant that Britomart and Artegall, the most powerful representatives of the two sides, will soon be united in mutual love and betrothal.

But the Tournament does not end in concord, as one would wish; rather the Snowy Florimell is judged the most beautiful, although she is clearly not the most virtuous (the prize girdle will not stay clasped around her, much to her own dismay and anger). And, allowed to select her own champion, she angers everyone by choosing Braggadochio, the one member of the troupe who most approximates her own virtues. This choice, then, disrupts the various alliances and sets us off on more adventures.

Like alliance, proximity can also sometimes be mistaken for friendship. When Paridell, Duessa, Blandamour, and Ate appear in canto i, they seem to be friends, but since theirs is a companionship based only on proximity, a factor even more transitory than alliance, at Ate's urging they soon break into open strife, including in their conflict Britomart and Scudamour, who have no real reason for enmity. Britomart's proximity to feuding makes her a part of that feud as well, through no fault of her own. If we do not choose our companions wisely, Spenser shows us, we are likely to fall prey to their flaws regardless of our own virtues. Britomart and Scudamour are certainly not of the same ilk as Paridell and Duessa, yet Ate, or Strife, is able to engage them as well, if only because they are there.

In the retrospective narrative of canto iii, we learn something of true friendship, but we also see that there is something magical, unpredictable about it. We learn that Triamond is the third of three brothers, sons of a mother who, like Cymoent, sought to protect her sons from harm. But her protection was limited to ensuring that the soul of any who died would be passed on to the next brother, thus allowing each to live in the others. Triamond is the surviving brother, and as such he possesses the souls of Priamond and Diamond, each of whom died at the hands of Cambell. The situation would hardly seem fit for an emblem of friendship. Cambell has killed Triamond's older brothers, and we would expect that chivalric codes of behavior would demand that Triamond seek revenge upon him.

But Cambina appears and settles the fight, like a deus ex machina in Greek drama. Her appearance and actions may be excessively artificial, certainly overtly allegorical, but we need such magic if we are to believe at all what happens, or even accept it. We must suspend our disbelief entirely and accept the magic, for without it we would continue to be suspicious that somehow one of the two knights would turn on the other, harboring a secret enmity. There are allegorical significances, of course, but Spenser is a good enough fiction writer to know that he must avoid false expectations that will stand in the reader's way of fully understanding the significance of the friendship between Cambell and Triamond. Furthermore, he seems clearly to be indicating that perfect concord between one-time enemies can only be achieved with some sort of infusion of magical *spirit,* if not by actual magic.

Something of that spirit is already present in the relationship of Britomart and Amoret, for in canto i, when Britomart reveals to Amoret that she is a woman, the two can become friends sharing a common goal, the search for their loved ones:

> And eke fayre Amoret now freed from feare,
> More franke affection did to her afford,
> And to her bed, which she was wont forbeare,
> Now freely drew, and found right safe assurance theare.

> Where all that night they of their loues did treat,
> And hard aduentures twixt themselues alone,
> That each the other gan with passion great,
> And griefull pietie priuately bemone.

> (IV.i.15–16)

Amoret at last has not only a champion who will be totally dependable, one who will not succumb to her beauty and fall to lust, but also a friend with whom she can share her innermost thoughts and fears.

We see a friendship between women with Britomart and Amoret, and between men with Cambell and Triamond, but we also see examples of friendship between men and women, including both platonic and nonplatonic relationships. In the reconciliation of Timias and Belphoebe we see an exemplum of friendship between man and woman, but a friendship completely devoid of sexuality. Timias earlier had loved, perhaps lusted after, Belphoebe, but his encounter with lust—and with Amoret—allows him to focus his friendship with Belphoebe, to realize that theirs is and must perforce be an entirely platonic relationship, one with which they can both be content. The episode that follows brings us two steps closer to the climactic reunion of Florimell and Marinell, for it involves not just the reuniting of Aemylia and her love Amyas, but also the new union between Placidas and Poeana, Amyas's captor. Here, then, we have both old love reunited and new love begun, emblems of Florimell's continuing love for Marinell and his newly discovered love for her in canto xii.

But before we can reach that final event, we must learn more of Amoret and Scudamour, particularly how Scudamour won his wife and came to be separated from her on their wedding day. This episode (in canto x) parallels cantos xi and xii of Book III, when Britomart rescues Amoret from the House of Busyrane. Now, at last, we learn more precisely how Amoret and Scudamour came to be married—and perhaps come better to understand how her fears were reflected in Busyrane's captivity.

Scudamour's account of how he gained Amoret by defeating 20 knights and winning the Shield of Love (a literal translation of his name), his key to entering the Temple of Venus, shows he is worthy of Amoret's love. At the same time, however, we should also be aware that Amoret, reared to be a perfect wife (as we have been told much earlier in III.vi), is little more than a prize for martial prowess, having no control over her own fate—and hence is overwhelmed by the fears of her own sexuality and of consummating the life for which she was reared, making her fit captive for Busyrane in Book III.

Amoret's concerns in the House of Busyrane episode of Book III are presented in a complex and mystifying allegorical episode. Scudamour's concerns are also presented allegorically, but in a more readily understood event, reminiscent of episodes in earlier books. We see his concerns in the House of Care, where Scudamour and Glauce attempt to rest in their continuing search for Amoret and Britomart. While the allegorical significance of the events of the House of Care may be rather heavy-handed (much like the figures in the Palace of Pride in Book I), they are at the same time examples of Spenser's use of psychological realism. The doubts about his love that Scudamour can suppress during his busy days invade his mind in the quiet of the night when he tries to sleep. Anyone who has ever spent a restless night knows precisely what Scudamour experiences:

> And euermore, when he to sleepe did thinke,
> > The hammers sound his senses did molest;
> And euermore, when he began to winke,
> > The bellowes noyse disturb'd his quiet rest,
> > Ne suffred sleepe to settle in his brest.
> > And all the night the dogs did barke and howle
> > About the house, at sent of stranger guest:
> > And now the crowing Cocke, and now the Owle
> Lowde shriking him afflicted to the very sowle.

> And if by fortune any little nap
> > Vpon his heauie eye-lids chaunst to fall,
> > Eftsoones one of those villeins him did rap
> > Vpon his headpeece with his yron mall;
> > That he was soone awaked therewithall,
> > And lightly started vp as one affrayd;
> > Or as if one him suddenly did call.
> > So oftentimes he out of sleepe abrayd,
> And then lay musing long, on that him ill apayd.
> > > > > > > (IV.v.41–42)

We have seen such psychologically realistic details before, and we also find in Book IV allegorical set pieces that remind us, for example, of Redcrosse's encounter in the Cave of Despair. There is, of course, the house of Sclaunder in canto viii, where Arthur travels with Amoret and Aemylia, who have just escaped from the Cave of Lust and are thus subject to slander, regardless of their innocence. In the earlier Cave of Lust episode of canto vi, we see personified lust in action, also reminiscent of personified Despair and his cave in Book I. And, again, we have the appearance of a character from an earlier episode, this time Timias, who wounds Amoret while rescuing her, and Belphoebe, who appropriately dispatches Lust only to find her friend, Timias, holding her twin sister, Amoret. Mistaking his care for a manifestation of the very lust she has just overcome, Belphoebe angrily leaves Timias to his own devices. The effects of lust, in other words, are not limited to lustful behavior, but to the appearance of such behavior as well. As long as lust can affect others, even those unaffected by it may fall prey to suspicion of lustfulness. His shame and her anger keep them separated, and only with the intervention of innocent nature—in the form of the bird—can Timias and Belphoebe be reconciled.

The final allegorical episode in this most episodic of the six books brings together its many themes, just as the marriage of the Thames and the Medway brings together the waters of the world. The last episode also parallels the House of Busyrane episode of Book III.xi–xii, for in the earlier book Amoret is held captive by a wall of flame, while in this book Florimell is held captive by a wall of water,[31] thus linking the potential reuniting of Scudamour and Amoret with the actual uniting and marriage of Florimell and Marinell.

The marriage of the rivers is an emblem of *discordia concors,* concord growing out of discord,[32] symbolized by the uniting of the rivers, which become one while maintaining their individual identities. One hesitates to ascribe such late-twentieth-century values to a poet of the 1590s, yet it seems clear that Spenser held at least a similar value, for the rivers do represent a marriage in which the partners become one entity, yet have maintained and will continue to maintain their individual importances and identities. We may not be able to tell which waters are which in their mingling, but we certainly still know that the Thames and the Medway must be merged to form a great whole—just as the individual Britomart and the individual Artegall must merge while at the same time maintaining their independent identities.

9

Book V:
The Legend of Justice

Book V returns to the form and structure of Books I and II, a single knight and his companion on a series of linked adventures presented in a straightforward narrative with only minimal diversions. But Book V presents its own problems, despite this return to the familiar, for the views Spenser allegorically presents here about the situation in Ireland are hardly compatible with modern tastes. As Secretary to Lord Grey, the Queen's Deputy in Ireland, Spenser was a government official involved in a policy of repression and slaughter. It is commonly accepted that in his harsher moments, especially when dealing with rebellion of various kinds, Artegall represents Lord Grey in his repressive treatment of the Irish. Spenser's apparent acceptance of this treatment, both in Book V of *The Faerie Queene* and in his *View of the present state of Ireland,* may have been acceptable to the English aristocracy of his own day, but leave him—quite justly, I believe—open to charges of supporting a tyrannous policy.

Examinations of Book V often seek to apologize for Spenser's attitudes, as if he were somehow a sixteenth-century version of the modern academic liberal in the other books but led innocently astray in this one. I don't subscribe to such a view. The historical situation Spenser portrays allegorically in Book V is, from our point of view, simply ugly. Such harsh repressive measures as Lord Grey took against the Irish are morally repugnant, and it is disturbing to admit that Spenser was involved in and approved of his actions. But he did, and to apologize for him, to make Book V somehow primarily reflective of higher moral concerns, is to deny the historical reality of Spenser's situation.

There is much more to this book, though, than just a political allegory portraying Lord Grey's role in Ireland, and it is those other elements to which we shall turn our attention. Meanwhile, however, the reader should rest assured that if parts of Book V seem frighteningly violent and morally reprehensible, that's because they are, and no amount of justification can make Spenser's role in this distasteful episode of English history any more attractive.

Unlike Books II, III, and IV, Book V does not begin with a major character from the previous book encountering the hero of the present book. Quite simply, this pattern is not necessary since we have been aware of Artegall since early in Book III, and we have seen him in action in Book IV. He is not new, nor do we need to see him in battle to prove his strength or wisdom. Rather, we learn of Artegall's background in a very straightforward narrative in the first part of canto i in which we are told that he was taken as a child by Astraea and trained by her in the ways of justice, which, under her tutelage, he practices on the beasts of the forest (like the young Achilles). His adventures in this book begin well after he has left the tutelage of Astraea, accompanied by Talus, the iron man she assigns to him as his companion.

As we have seen throughout *The Faerie Queene*, we are watching the education of the various heroes and a progression from the very personal toward the increasingly public—from Holiness in Book I to Friendship in Book IV. Book V continues this progression by focusing on Justice, the extension of codified rules of individual behavior to society as a whole through the enforcement of law and equity.

Artegall's training in the ways of justice by Astraea has been theoretical, and his only practice has been on the beasts of the forest. He has learned the use of force, we must presume, for even in this allegorical world the wild beasts are not subject to logic and rhetoric, nor are their situations at all ambiguous, so his decisions presumably have been easy ones. Now, as we watch, Artegall's decisions will become increasingly more difficult, less dependent upon received wisdom and the force of previous law—less dependent, in other words, upon precedent and more dependent upon his own ability to decide wisely, to bring the weight of his own experience and intellect to bear upon more difficult issues.

In English law until the late nineteenth century, two systems of courts existed side by side: one the normal courts of law, which enforced written statutes, and the other, designed to prevent inequities in legal matters, the courts of equity. The latter were presided over by the Court of Chancery—and one of Spenser's positions was as Registrar to the Faculties in the Court of Chancery in Dublin. The Court of Equity, briefly, existed to prevent injustices in the law. Its function was to provide "recourse to general principles of justice . . . to correct or supplement the provisions of the law." Courts of Equity had the power to overrule decisions by the courts of law and dealt with cases "for which the law did not provide adequate remedy or in which its operations would have been unfair."[33] In Book V, Artegall must learn the role of equity in bringing justice to society, to temper justice with mercy, and to distinguish true mercy from mere pity.

This is not just the education of a young knight in the ways of the law, but rather the progression of Artegall from a young "prelaw student" to the position of wise "judge," one who can deal with all issues of justice. If we think of Artegall and his adventures in these terms, we can better understand the progression of Book V, for in it he moves through increasingly knottier legal issues through the first three and one-half cantos, then falls prey to Radigund in the middle third of the book, a result of ill-placed pity, and in the final third puts his thorough understanding of law, mercy, and equity to work in a series of adventures that allegorically portray events of Spenser's own day.

Artegall's first adventure once he has left Astraea's guidance involves a precedent so well known as to be almost a cliché, the judgment of Solomon. In that judgment, Solomon must determine which of two women is the mother of a living child and which the mother of a dead child. He determines the rightful mother by suggesting that they "Deuide . . . the liuing childe in twaine, and giue the one halfe to the one, and the other halfe to the other." The mother of the dead child, of course, is content with the solution, having nothing more to lose, but the mother of the living child says "vnto the King, for her compassion was kindled toward her sonne & she said, Oh my lord, giue her the liuing childe and slay him not."[34]

Artegall's situation is precisely that of Solomon: he must decide between two men who provide antithetical evidence with no outside corroboration (given the subordinate legal situation of women in sixteenth-century England, we should not wonder why the woman is not consulted). Artegall decides the case absolutely according to precedent: offering to divide the living and the dead women equally between the two men and thus provoking a withdrawal from the innocent squire. There are several points of interest in this episode, however, that show us something about Artegall's education and Spenser's views. Most important, Spenser does not necessarily intend us to see that Artegall is as wise as Solomon; indeed, to pattern one's judgment after an earlier case is intelligent legal action, but in such an obvious situation it is more a sign of adequate training than brilliance. Furthermore, Artegall knows already one of the most powerful rhetorical tools of the attorney: equivocation. He does not specifically say that he will divide the living woman in half; rather, he merely suggests that "both the dead and liuing equally / Deuided be betwixt you here in sight, / And each of either take his share aright" (V.i.26). The two litigants, of course, assume that he means to divide the living woman, and thus he provokes the response he expects. It seems reasonable, however, to assume that Artegall means to give the dead woman to one man, the living to the other; the "share aright" is what must be determined. Even if the knight and the squire agree to this suggestion, Artegall has placed himself under no obligation to divide the living woman between them. In other words, Artegall begins this book knowledgeable in the ways of justice, and already a subtle jurist.

It is, however, especially interesting to note the shift from earlier to more modern forms of justice in this canto. The squire, although he knows himself to be in the right, declines the most direct and primitive form of proof, trial by arms:

> Well did that Squire perceiue him selfe too weake,
>   To aunswere his defiaunce in the field,
>   And rather chose his challenge off to breake,
>   Then to approue his right with speare and shield.
>   And rather guilty chose him selfe to yield.
>
> (V.i.24)

Trial by arms clearly favors the stronger, better equipped, better trained disputant and thus by even the wildest stretch of imagination could only be considered "fair" if the two litigants are of equal strength and stature. (One thinks, for example, of Bullingbrook and Mowbray in the first act of Shakespeare's *Richard II,* two combatants who are surely of equal strength and stature and thus capable of settling their issue at least fairly if not accurately.) Law has an equalling effect; it is necessary to protect the innocent weaker against the guilty stronger. As Spenser shows us by having trial by arms rejected early in this book, justice reaches beyond mere might; it is indeed protection for the weak against the mighty.

But law, of course, is also an extension of such might—here in the form of Talus, the iron man who does Artegall's bidding: he is the strong, if not long, arm of the law. In effect, Artegall issues a warrant for Sanglier and sends Talus to serve it: "No sooner sayd, but streight he after sent / His yron page, who him pursew'd so light, / As that it seem'd aboue the ground he went (V.i.20).

Talus's power is absolute, but like idealized law it is clearly also under the control of Artegall (and thus Talus will be unable to act later when Artegall is held captive by Radigund).

The squire's rejection of armed combat with Sanglier indicates that we are dealing with a new kind of justice, a justice necessary, perhaps, in the fallen world that Spenser laments in the proem to Book V. Artegall must turn to more sophisticated forms of determining the truth. His proposal for discovering the truth sets forth the situation succinctly:

> Now sure this doubtfull causes right
> Can hardly but by Sacrament be tride,
> Or else by ordele, or by bloody fight;
> That ill perhaps mote fall to either side,
> But if ye please, that I your cause decide,
> Perhaps I may all futher quarrell end,
> So ye will sweare my judgment to abide.
>
> (V.i.25)

He recognizes, as society must recognize, that the "traditional" methods of proving innocence or guilt are inherently unfair. Trial by sacrament—that is, by swearing an oath—can hardly be effective against one willing to perjure or blaspheme; trial by ordeal—that is, by fire or water—may well result in injury to an innocent party. And, of course, trial by combat clearly favors a knight over a squire. Given the decline of such traditional methods, more suited to a golden than a stone age, society must, as Artegall indicates, agree to select from among its numbers a wise judge and to abide by that judge's carefully weighed decisions.

Artegall's second adventure finds him faced with somewhat knottier problems with far more unpleasant outcomes. In canto i he must deal with what is essentially a civil issue—a dispute between two parties, each of whom claims (and on the surface appears to have) equal right to "property" (if we may be so crass as to refer to the poor woman in question in these terms). In canto ii, the disputes are between public and private rights.

On first reading, the two major events of canto ii—the defeat of Pollente and Munera and of the Giant—appear to be completely unrelated issues, linked only by the narrative structure of Artegall's travels. They are, however, closely linked in another way, for the former represents the conflict created by those who would make public property private and the latter the conflict created by those who would make private property public. In modern terms, Spenser is dealing with the excesses of capitalism and communism.

Pollente has built or commandeered a bridge, a crucial part of the public right-of-way, and exacts a toll for its use. How he acquired it is not clear. The toll Pollente charges is absolute: the life and goods of those who try to use his bridge. Thus he impinges upon the public right-of-way for private gain, growing wealthy by controlling something—the right to passage over the river and gorge—that should be public and free. Furthermore, he resorts to trickery to defeat those who would cross the gorge, winning clear advantage by the trapdoor in the middle of the bridge.

Artegall is able to defeat him, not because of his inherent superiority of intellect or arms, but rather because he knows in advance of the trapdoor that gives Pollente such a powerful advantage over his enemies. Having been informed by Dony, Florimell's dwarf, about the trapdoor, when it opens "he was well aware, and leapte before his fall" (V.ii.12), thus turning Pollente's advantage against him, surprising the evil knight with his knowledge, and defeating him in their battle in the river. Artegall beheads Pollente and posts his head on the bridge, a fitting end for one who has used the bridge so dishonorably, but also a clear allusion to the Elizabethan practice of posting the heads of traitors on London Bridge. Artegall dedicates the bridge to public use when he repairs it after Pollente's death.

Talus's defeat of Pollente's daughter, Munera, seems particularly harsh, for he cuts off her hands and feet, then throws her screaming to her death in the river below the castle walls. Gruesome it may be, but it is also appropriate, for she represents not just wealth accumulated by illegal and immoral means, but also attempted bribery of the legal arm, for she quite literally showers Talus with wealth when he is attempting to gain entry to her castle:

> But when as yet she saw him to proceede,
>> Vnmou'd with praiers, or with piteous thought,
>> She ment him to corrupt with goodly meede;
>> And causde great sackes with endlesse riches fraught,
>> Vnto the battilment to be vpbrought,
>> And powred forth ouer the Castle wall,
>> That she might win some time, though dearly bought
>> Whilest he to gathering of the gold did fall.
> But he was nothing mou'd nor tempted therewithall.
>
> (V.ii.23)

Pollente, then, represents those who would turn the rights of the public to their own benefit—and Munera the bribery such villains must resort to if they are to get their way. Their punishment is harsh because they represent threats to the very fabric of society; if they are allowed to succeed, society will offer no benefits to the bulk of its citizens, and if they are not severely and publicly punished, others will not be fully aware of the ends to which such actions can lead. Similarly, the castle must be razed and the servants routed to make unequivocally clear that no benefits may derive from such actions.

But having made clear that the rights of the public must be protected, Spenser demonstrates that there are also limits on those rights, that the public should not have unlimited access to private property. The Giant with his scales represents the obverse of Pollente and Munera. In his attempt to equalize all things, including nature, the Giant is as much a threat to the fabric of society as Pollente and Munera, for if there are no private rewards and private property, if indeed all are absolutely equal, then society as Spenser and his contemporaries knew it is bound to fail. The Giant and his rabble must be defeated. Artegall attempts to deal with the Giant rationally, to persuade him before resorting to force. But rhetoric fails, and when it does, the harsh action of the law must come into play in the form of the unrelenting Talus, who tosses the Giant over the cliff to his death on the rocky seashore below, then defeats the rabble, the crowd rising up in revolt because it has been led to expect great wealth at the expense of private property. (It is worth noting, incidentally, that the deaths in this canto all involve falling from high places, an apt metaphor for the fall of the mighty who have achieved their status at the expense of society.)

Cantos iii and iv continue the increasingly sophisticated legal issues Artegall must deal with. In the tournament for the marriage of Florimell and Marinell in canto iii, several familiar characters appear once more, and, at last, Braggadochio and his companion Trompart receive punishment appropriate to the crimes they have committed since their first appearance in Book II, exposed for the lying cowards they really are. Talus shaves Braggadochio's beard, breaks his sword, and paints over the coat of arms on his shield, making clear his true cowardly nature and bringing to a close his participation in *The Faerie Queene*. The Snowy Florimell, her falseness revealed at last by Artegall, melts away entirely, thus ending her adventures, which began in Book III. Artegall intercedes between Guyon and Braggadochio because, as we have seen, trial by arms is no longer appropriate, and he calls—for the first time—for an external and living witness, albeit that witness is Guyon's horse. Artegall has become sufficiently sophisticated that he is at least able to expose blatant hypocrisy and false beauty and to begin to call upon witnesses. He may not yet be a perfect judge, but he is well on his way, making decisions for which there is no clear precedent, even if those decisions are relatively easy to make. His legal methodology will continue to grow in sophistication in the following canto when he must call upon the laws of nature to rule on a case.

His next decision requires him to have a clear knowledge of international legal practices, for he must settle a dispute between the brothers Amidas and Bracidas, who are fighting over their patrimony and dowry, both of which have been altered by the actions of the sea. The law of the sea, Artegall says, is clear, and that is what must govern this case:

> For what the mighty Sea hath once possest,
> And plucked quite from all possessors hand,
> Whether by rage of waues, that neuer rest,
> Or else by wracke, that wretches hath distrest,
> He may dispose by his imperiall might,
> As thing at random left, to whom he list.
>
> (V.iv.19)

This decision has led Artegall to a far more sophisticated legal position. He began his legal career merely replicating the judgment of Solomon, and by canto iv he is in position to litigate a case involving not just human law, but the laws of nature as well. But merely understanding the law is not sufficient. If he is indeed to be the Knight of Justice in the fullest sense, he must also learn the role of equity and thus must learn the difference between misdirected pity and true mercy.

The first four and one-half cantos of Book V deal with Artegall's legal education, bringing him to the point that he is now ready to make his first major error as a judge. Failing to recognize that the law must stand above mere human emotion, he allows inappropriate pity to overcome his knowledge and training. He must now learn that although mercy has an important place in the role of justice, pity should not. He falls victim to Radigund because he is overcome by pity when he sees that she is a beautiful young woman:

> At sight thereof his cruell minded hart
>   Empierced was with pittifull regard,
>   That his sharpe sword he threw from him apart,
>   Cursing his hand that had that visage mard.
>
> (V.v.13)

His failure to execute Radigund may momentarily seem an admirable action; after all, it clearly parallels his reaction in Book IV when he first realizes that Britomart is a woman. But pity in personal relationships and pity in legal situations are two quite different things, as Artegall learns to his dismay. When Radigund awakens from her swoon and takes him captive, we realize that pity has served Artegall ill, that justice has failed because it placed pity before the law, and thus Artegall reaches the low point of his career, dressed in women's clothes and working at a spinning wheel.

Like other major characters of *The Faerie Queene*, he has lost control of his own powers and must be rescued if he is to continue his quest. That rescue comes at the hands not of Arthur as it does for the heroes of other books, but of his beloved Britomart, who has learned of his plight from Talus. Talus, iron man though he may be, approaches Britomart with the greatest of trepidation in what may be the only touch of comedy in all of Book V:

> The yron man, albe he wanted sence
> And sorrowes feeling, yet with conscience
> Of his ill newes, did inly chill and quake,
> And stood still mute, as one in great suspence
> As if that by his silence he would make
> Her rather reade his meaning, then him selfe it spake.
>
> (V.vi.9)

"*Talus* be bold," she orders him—following the advice she learned at the House of Busyrane (but he, it is clear, would prefer that other advice: "Be not too bold"). When Talus does reveal Artegall's whereabouts, Britomart shows her human side, suspecting the worst and rebuking the messenger: "Cease thou bad newes-man, badly does thou hide / Thy maisters shame, in harlots bondage tide" (V.vi.11).

The iron man explains the entire situation to her, but before she can rescue her betrothed, Britomart needs confirmation that he is indeed worthy of rescue; that confirmation she finds at the Temple of Isis in canto vii.

Falling asleep in the Temple, Britomart experiences a horrifying dream, a vision that parallels and completes those she has experienced in her adventures in Books III and IV. Her white linen robe turns blood red, a crocodile first tries to attack her, then becomes her lover, and she gives birth to a lion. Awakening, she goes to a priest for help and he, knowing who she really is, explains the symbolism of the dream:

she will help tame Artegall's might, marry him, and give birth to a royal son. Combined with Artegall, in effect, she will not only become perfect Chastity but also help create perfect justice by tempering its might with clemency to produce "that part of Iustice, which is Equity" (V.vii.3).

Knowing her full role and understanding her relationship with Artegall, Britomart may now rescue him and free him to continue in his duties. She defeats Radigund and frees Artegall. While Artegall continues on his adventure, then, Britomart remains behind at Radigund's castle, freeing the knights who have been enthralled to the evil former ruler, reminding us of Elizabeth's reign after the terrors of her sister Mary:

> she there as princess rained,
> And changing all that forme of common weale,
> The liberty of women did repeale,
> Which they had long vsurpt; and them restoring
> To mens subiection, did true Iustice deale:
> That all they as a Goddesse her adoring,
> Her wisedome did admire, and hearkned to her loring.
>
> For all those Knights, which long in captiue shade
> Had shrowded bene, she did from thraldome free;
> And magistrates of all that city made,
> And gaue to them great liuing and large fee:
> (V.vii.42–43)

But she is not Elizabeth but rather a woman betrothed, and thus she makes the newly freed knights swear fealty to Artegall rather than to herself. There is, however, another allegorical significance to this scene, for Britomart's rescue of Artegall represents another level of justice: the freeing of an unjustly imprisoned man, and thus the freeing of justice itself, both in the person of Artegall and in the abstract.

Artegall's next adventure takes him into the realm of foreign policy, for together with Prince Arthur he must rescue the Queen Mercilla from the unwanted and unlawful advances of the Souldan and his wife. Like Guyon and the Redcrosse Knight in Book II, Artegall and Arthur begin their companionship by threatening each other. Unlike the earlier heroes, though, Artegall and Arthur actually come to blows, each thinking he is rescuing Samient, Mercilla's servant, from the other. But they are so equal in might and skill that neither can dismount the other:

> so both anon
> Together met, and strongly either strooke
> And broke their speares; yet neither has forgon
> His horses backe, yet to and fro long shooke,
> And tottered like two towres, which through a tempest quooke.
>
> (V.viii.9)

Samient prevents their fighting further, pointing out that they have already slain their foes—and hers—thus making them appropriately allies. They make peace at her suggestion and agree to unite in avenging the Souldan's treatment of Mercilla.

The Souldan episode is commonly taken to represent Philip II of Spain's attempts to conquer England. His hooked chariot may be, as Hamilton points out, a symbolic representation of Spanish battleships, which were "headed with yron, and hooked on the sides."[35] Allegorically, such an interpretation is both acceptable and consistent, for Philip was seen as posing a threat to England, and the routing of the Souldan and his chariot by Arthur certainly parallels the effects of the weather—the meteorological manifestation of God's Grace—in destroying Philip's armada and dashing his hopes of conquest against the treacherous rocks of the English seacoast.

At the same time, however, another near-contemporary figure may have provided Spenser with his actual model—indeed even his title—for the Souldan and his wife: Süleyman the Magnificent, Sultan of the Ottoman Empire, who reigned from 1520 to 1566. One of his wives, Roxelana, like the Souldan's wife, was noted for her ferocity, having convinced her husband to kill one of his older sons so her own son could be next in line for this throne. This pair would seem, then, to make a worthy model for the Souldan and his tigress of a wife, and the victory of Artegall and Arthur is meant to represent not only the English defeat of the Spanish, but also the superiority of Christian warriors over the "pagan" Süleyman as well.

With this episode, Artegall's adventures turn toward what is clearly historical allegory dealing with events of Spenser's own day and attempting to justify both Lord Grey's treatment of the Irish rebels and larger issues of Elizabeth's domestic and foreign policies.

Before they continue to Mercilla's palace, Artegall and Arthur agree to destroy Malengin, the personification of guile. They try to capture him by guileful means, but of course cannot for he is in his home territory—and playing by his own rules. Not until Artegall un-leashes Talus, in fact, have they even a hope of capturing him. When Talus captures Malengin and hands him to Artegall, however, the villain turns himself into a prickly hedgehog, escaping once more. Recaptured, he turns himself into a snake, and Talus beats him to death, allowing no further transformations and bringing the issue to a close.

Allegorically, the episode may teach us (and Artegall) that the absolute force of the law is required against guileful opponents; when such a criminal is brought before a judge by the arm of the law, he may make his escape by appearing to be something quite different from what he really is and thus must be treated most forcefully by the law during the capture. More important, though, Malengin may also represent the Irish rebels, particularly given Spenser's portrait of his filthy, rustic, unkempt appearance. Because the rebels could appear to be innocent, the only solution to the Irish rebellion, Lord Grey had suggested, is their total and absolute destruction. And here Spenser would seem clearly to concur with such a policy.

Malengin's punishment is fit for the crimes he has committed, and there is no sense that any character in *The Faerie Queene* (or perhaps many readers among Spenser's English contemporaries) would think it unfitting. In the remainder of this canto, however, Spenser deals

allegorically with a contemporary political issue about which there was
much debate and doubt: the execution of Mary Queen of Scots by her
cousin, the Queen. The second half of canto ix concentrates on the
trial and execution of Duessa, the personification of duplicity whom
we first met early in Book I, and who still continues to fool some:

> Then was there brought, as prisoner to the barre,
>   A Ladie of great countenance and place,
>   But that she it with foule abuse did marre;
>   Yet did appeare rare beautie in her face,
>   But blotted with condition vile and base
>   That all her other honour did obscure,
>   And titles of nobilitie deface:
>   Yet in that wretched semblant, she did sure
> The peoples great compassion vnto her allure.
>
>   (V.ix.38)

There is little doubt that Duessa represents Mary Queen of Scots here:
even Mary's son, James VI of Scotland (and the future James I of
England) recognized the portrait and demanded (to no avail) that
Spenser be punished for it. Spenser takes great pains in this episode to
justify the execution of Duessa by Mercilla—and hence his queen's
role in the execution of her cousin. He points particularly (in more
than just her name) to the mercy and compassion felt by Mercilla:

> But she, whose Princely breast was touched nere
>   With piteous ruth of her so wretched plight,
>   Though plaine she saw by all, that she did heare,
>   That she of death was guiltie found by right,
>   Yet would not let iust vengeance on her light;
>   But rather let in stead thereof to fall
>   Few perling drops from her faire lampes of light;
>   The which she couering with her purple pall
> Would haue the passion hid, and vp arose withall.
>
>   (V.ix.50)

It is also clear, however, that while Mercilla personally has compassion for Duessa, in her political role she must carry out the requirements of the law. But Spenser delays the event until the following canto, a pause that parallels Elizabeth's own delay in executing Mary. Finally, however, justice overcomes pity and Duessa is put to death. This may well be the episode for which Spenser has been preparing us throughout Book V, for Artegall clearly sees that the execution is necessary, a view he simply could not have shared before he had been captured by Radigund as a result of his misguided pity. Furthermore, we have seen even in this very canto that some guile—and duplicity is the most grievous form of that vice—cannot be defeated except by the most extreme methods. The execution of Duessa, accepted by Arthur and Artegall "when they had seene and heard her doom a rights" (V.x.4), justifies the execution of Mary Queen of Scots as well.

Cantos x, xi, and xii offer together a justification of English foreign policy under Elizabeth's reign, specifically policies regarding the conflicts with the Spanish, represented by Gereoneo and Grantorto (i.e., Philip of Spain) in the Netherlands (Belge), France (Burbon), and Ireland (Irena). Spenser here expands the role of justice to the international realm, moving from merely repelling invaders in Mercilla's kingdom to justifying using one's forces in foreign nations. Arthur goes in aid of Belge, who has sent two of her sons to Mercilla seeking aid against the tyrannical Gereoneo, whose role in Belge's kingdom resembles Philip's role in the Low Countries, where he was called in as a protector but (from the English point of view at least) ruled as a tyrant. In canto x Arthur defeats Gereoneo's knights and restores Belge to her castle, then in the following canto he defeats Gereoneo himself, restores Belge to her throne, then destroys the beast that has taken her church, presumably a representation of the effects of the Inquisition in the Netherlands.

In the second half of canto xi, we turn our attention back to Artegall, who continues on his quest to rescue Irena. On his way, however, he encounters Burbon, rescues him from a rabble aroused in support of Grantorto, and agrees to restore him to his lady, Flourdelis.

On the simplest allegorical level, Burbon represents Henry IV of France, who had given up his protestant religion in order to return to Paris and who was beseiged by supporters of Philip of Spain. Burbon attempts to justify laying aside the shield given him by the Redcrosse Knight; it is, he says, just a temporary measure, and he may take up the shield again when it serves his purposes, but Artegall reprimands him for such fickle behavior:

> Fie on such forgerie (said *Artegall*)
> Vnder one hood to shadow faces twaine.
> Knights ought be true, and truth is one in all:
> Of all things to dissemble fouly may befall.
>
> (V.xi.56)

Nonetheless, Artegall agrees to help restore Burbon to Flourdelis and, that task accomplished, continues to his final adventure, a further (and more explicit) justification of Lord Grey's policies in Ireland.

In canto xii Artegall defeats Grantorto, chopping off his head, and restores Irena to her people, but his victory is not complete, for like Lord Grey, he is recalled to Court, leaving his task unfinished:

> But ere he could reforme it thoroughly,
> He through occasion called was away,
> To Faerie Court, that of necessity
> His course of Iustice he was forst to stay,
> And *Talus* to reuoke from the right way,
> In which he was that Realme for to redresse.
> But enuies cloud still dimmeth vertues ray.
> So hauing freed Irena from distresse,
> He tooke his leaue of her, there left in heauinesse.
>
> (V.xii.27)

This book, then, distinguishes itself significantly from the earlier books by its ending, for although Artegall has been victorious in his quest, he has not been wholly successful. Rather than a celebration of his might and victory, in the final third of canto xii he meets with Envy and

Detraction and their horrid companion: "A monster, which the *Blatant beast* men call, / A dreadfull feend of gods and men ydrad, / Whom they by slights allur'd, and to their purpose lad" (V.xii.37).

Their attack on Artegall is unrelenting, but he ignores them, continuing on his way to Court—and thus ending this book on a sad, even sour note, reflective of Spenser's own view of the fate of his patron, Lord Grey, who was dismissed by Queen Elizabeth. The ending, further, helps us better understand the very beginning of this book, the proem, in which Spenser laments the changing of the world from golden to stone:

> So oft as I with state of present time,
>> The image of the antique world compare,
>> When as mans age was in his freshest prime,
>> And the first blossome of faire vertue bare,
>> Such oddes I finde twixt those, and these which are,
>> As that, through long continuance of his course,
>> Me seems the world is runne quite out of square,
>> From the first point of his appointed sourse,
> And being once amisse growes daily wourse and wourse.
>
> For from the golden age, that first was named,
>> It's now at earst become a stonie one;
>> And men themselues, the which at first were framed
>> Of earthly mould, and form'd of flesh and bone,
>> Are now transformed into hardest stone:
>> Such as behind their backs (so backward bred)
>> Were throwne by Pyrrha and Deucalione:
>> And if then those may any worse be red
> They into that ere long will be engendered.
>
> (V.p.1–2)

10

Book VI:
The Legend of Courtesie

Many readers have remarked on the shift in tone that occurs as we leave the world of Book V and enter that of Book VI. There is a sense in which we shift from the harshness of justice and its demands to the rich patterns of pastoral romance. But to see only the contrast between these two books is to disregard Spenser's ongoing plan for *The Faerie Queene*. Book VI is not, strictly speaking, a departure from Book V; rather it is the next stage in Spenser's education of the gentleman or noble person. Having learned the necessity of justice and equity to society's survival, the reader must now turn to courtesy, a virtue necessary for society's well-being. If justice is common morality codified, the rules governing basic human behavior, then courtesy is equity internalized, the source of behavior that assures human beings can live in harmony and concord.

While Book VI continues Spenser's programmatic intention, it also departs significantly from the earlier books. It is, first of all, somewhat less allegorical. Personified abstractions and other overtly allegorical figures make fewer appearances in this book, and historical allegory seems almost entirely to have gone by the boards, although cases can be (and have been) made for Sir Philip Sidney or the Earl of Essex as models for Calidore. More important, though, Calidore is alone among Spenser's heroes in having no companion, a condition he laments when he tells Artegall that even if he is successful, "yet shall it not by none be testifyde" (VI.i.6). Calidore must learn that courtesy is its own reward; it does not require—nor should one expect—overt recognition from others for courteous behavior. Calidore also differs from earlier characters in being the only one of Spenser's heroes to consciously abandon his quest. He is not, like the Redcrosse Knight, misled by a villain, but rather succumbs to a life of ease, to the joys of pastoral existence—and the beauty of Pastorella. He is brought back on track only by external circumstances, the invasion of the Brigands and the utter destruction of the "ideal" pastoral world to which he has retreated. Furthermore, when he does return to his quest, his success is at best only partial, for the Blatant Beast, the object of his quest, will soon escape and be as much of a threat as ever.

Nonetheless, in the adventures of Book VI, we come to know what courtesy is and to realize that it is far more complex than we are led to believe at the outset. Spenser opens canto i of Book VI by indicating that courtesy is found, if not exclusively, at least most readily in courtly surroundings. More important, however, he begins with an etymological definition of the concept of courtesy:

> Of Court it seemes, men Courtesie doe call,
>> For that it there most vseth to abound;
>> And wel beseemeth that in Princes hall
>> That vertue should be plentifully found,
>> Which of all goodly manners is the ground,
>> And roote of ciuill conuersation.
>> Right so in Faery court it did redound,
>> Where curteous Knights and Ladies most did won
> Of all on earth, and made a matchlesse paragon.
>
> (VI.i.1)

Having established the origins of the word in the court, he then shows us its manifestation in a paragon of the virtue, Sir Calidore, who embodies all three facets of courtesy covered in this book: the natural qualities ("gentlenesse of spright/And manners mylde"), the fruits of study, particularly linguistic facility ("gracious speach"), and, finally, knightly training (he is "well approu'd in batteilous affray") (VI.i.2).

The first third of the book concentrates largely on what may be perceived as the most complex and formalized type of courtesy, that which Calidore exhibits from the outset, chivalric behavior. The middle cantos concentrate primarily on courtesy as enacted by other upper-class characters. But in cantos ix–xii we see that courtesy extends beyond the court and courtly behavior and can be found even among more lowly members of society. Spenser demonstrates that while "courtesy" may derive from "court," and courtly behavior, it is not restricted to members of the upper classes. Spenser has not said that all who reside in court are courteous, but only that it "wel *beseemeth* that" courtesy should be found there.

The book opens with courtly and chivalric figures in whom courtesy is manifest, Calidore and Calepine, who presumably have the advantages of both training and birth; Tristram, who has noble birth, is also courteous, although he has not yet had chivalric training and thus must become Calidore's squire (if only *in absentia*). Furthermore, such behavior is also manifested in the Salvage Man, who lacks not only noble birth and chivalric training, but even language, being restricted to "a soft murmure, and confused sound / Of senselesse words, which nature did him teach" (VI.iv.ii). Members of all social classes can behave courteously—after all, even the brigand captain exhibits some elements of courteous behavior in protecting Pastorella from the slave dealers.

Perhaps only those who have the advantages of both birth and training can truly embody courtesy in its highest forms, for there it involves both courtly and chivalric behavior. But this is not to say that others should not strive for the ideal or that they cannot learn modes of behavior from it. The lower classes are obliged to emulate their betters insofar as they can, and the upper classes have an obligation to be good models of courteous behavior. Thus there are dangers in

Calidore's giving over to the pastoral life; he becomes a less than complete model of such behavior, relinquishing the chivalric portion of his courtesy to become a temporary shepherd, and he is resoundingly criticized for his lapse:

> Who now does follow the foule *Blatant Beast,*
>   Whilest *Calidore* does follow that faire Mayd,
>   Vnmyndfull of his vow and high beheast,
>   Which by the Faery Queene was on him layd,
>   That he should neuer leaue, nor be delayd
>   From chacing him, till he had it attchieued?
>   But now entrapt of loue, which him betrayd,
>   He mindeth more, how he may be relieued
> With grace from her, whose loue his heart hath sore
> engrieued.
>
> (VI.x.i)

Calidore's abandoning of his quest is one form of discourtesy, a failure to perform his duty, to keep his promise to maintain a course of action. Book VI abounds with examples of other forms of discourteous behavior, ranging from those whose trespass is more an annoyance than a danger, through those whose actions imperil others, to the object of Calidore's quest, the ultimate embodiment of such behavior,

> the *Blatant Beast,*
>   a wicked Monster, that his tongue doth whet
>   Gainst all, both good and bad, both most and least,
>   And poures his poysnous gall forth to infest
>   The noblest wights with notable defame:
>   Ne euer Knight, that bore so lofty creast,
>   Ne euer Lady of so honest name
> But he them spotted with reproch, or secrete shame.
>
> (VI.vi.12)

The book begins, though, with a positive example of courteous behavior and, particularly, the importance of speech to such courtesy.

As with earlier books, the hero of Book VI begins his adventures by meeting the hero of the previous book. In Book II, as we have seen, the meeting between Guyon and Redcrosse nearly results in a fight, and in Book III Britomart and Guyon actually do fight. In this book, however, the meeting between Calidore and Artegall begins courteously—with talk. There is no sense whatsoever of the potential animosity that marks the openings of Books II and III. The Book of Courtesy begins, as true courtesy begins, with polite speech, each knight inquiring after the other's quest and treating the other with respect. From this polite and courteous beginning, Spenser leads us through a progression of episodes demonstrating increasingly discourteous and correspondingly more dangerous behavior.

After separating from Artegall, Calidore encounters a pair of foes whose discourtesy takes a form more insulting than dangerous. Although their servant Maleffort is dangerous enough, Crudor and Briana themselves are not horrid physical threats: they merely shave people, disgracing them, perhaps, but not killing or otherwise harming them. The hair and beard will, after all, grow back. Crudor and Briana, then, would seem to represent open affrontery, defiance essentially for its own sake.[36] They are, simply put, rude, and their rudeness is more offensive than dangerous, causing temporary discomfort and shame, to be sure, but no longer-lasting ill effects. It is appropriate, then, that once Calidore has conquered Crudor and extracted a promise of better behavior from him and Briana, there need be no further punishment. The discourteous behavior has been corrected, those affected by it released. The episode even has a happy ending, for Crudor and Briana are not only reformed, but united.

The opening two events of Book VI, then, may be said to be mirror images, the first an example of courteous talk, the second of discourteous—insulting—talk.[37] The mirrors of behavior continue throughout the book, building on a series of contrastive behaviors, which, taken together, show us the various extremes that must be avoided or encompassed to achieve courtesy in its fullest sense.

In canto ii, Calidore meets Tristram, an untrained youth who nonetheless exhibits true chivalric behavior. Although Calidore reprimands Tristram for violating the code of chivalric behavior in killing a knight and thus violating "the law of armes" (VI.ii.7), we soon learn that the violation was justified, for Tristram's victim has himself violated the same code in attacking and injuring the unarmed Aladine. Tristram and the unnamed knight he kills are mirror images: unarmored, Tristram kills a fully armored knight; the knight, in full armor, earlier attempted to kill an unarmed knight. Justice is served by coming full circle—and appropriate behavior is shown in the untrained youth while it is violated in the trained knight. Training, it seems clear, is insufficient to guarantee courteous behavior, and a lack of training may not prevent true chivalric behavior.

In the second half of canto ii Calidore meets Priscilla and the wounded Aladine and demonstrates another form of courtesy, which will be mirrored in canto iii. Priscilla, although too polite to ask for help, is desperate for aid; Calidore offers his help, demonstrating that the truly courteous person recognizes need even when it is not articulated. The mere fact that someone needs help should be sufficient reason to offer it. When Calidore takes Aladine and Priscilla to the home of Aldus, Aladine's father, Aldus, demonstrates another facet of true courtesy: age, weakness, or even grief should not stand in the way of treating houseguests well:

> So well and wisely did that good old Knight
> Temper his griefe, and turned it to cheare,
> To cheare his guests, whom he had stayd that night
> And make their welcome to them well appeare.
> (VI.iii.6)

When he takes Priscilla home to her father, Calidore essentially lies to save her reputation, claiming that she is "most perfect pure, and guiltlesse innocent / Of blame, as he did on his Knighthood sweare, / Since first he saw her" (VI.iii.18). True, he lies by omission rather than commission, and his careful choice of language allows him to equivocate (saying she has been innocent "since first he saw her"). Nonetheless, Spenser illustrates here that there are times when strict adherence to the absolute truth may stand in the way of truly courteous behavior; a judicious use of language may serve one well in such circumstances.

The second half of this canto turns to a parallel story with a quite different outcome: the relationship of Calepine and Serena. Like the earlier couple, Calepine and Serena have been approached unaware at a delicate and embarrassing moment. But while Priscilla is spared true danger and damage to her reputation, Serena is not. Wandering alone in the wood, she is attacked by the Blatant Beast, while her lover and Sir Calidore exchange stories of knightly adventures. That the episodes are parallel and Serena's trespass no greater than Priscilla's should make us question why the latter's reputation goes untarnished while Serena is attacked and wounded by the Beast, the embodiment of scandal. The reason is not entirely clear; it may be merely a matter of chance or a matter of specific circumstance: Serena wanders off alone, totally unprotected and undisturbed by the potential of danger, while Calepine and Calidore most discourteously ignore her to attend to their own (male) talk. (One is reminded of teenage boys discussing sports to the exclusion of their female companions.)

From this point through canto viii, the focus of the narrative shifts from Calidore to Calepine and Serena and their adventures, particularly with Turpine and Blandina, a couple parallel to Crudor and Briana from canto i. While Crudor and Briana were not, however, particularly dangerous and their behavior was subject to reform, this new pair is both dangerous and irredeemable. Turpine and Blandina may, in fact, represent the two extreme forms of discourtesy, he being total and obvious discourtesy, or turpitude, she being skilled in using rhetoric to disguise her manipulativeness:

> For well she knew the wayes to win good will
> Of euery wight, that were not too infest
> And how to please the minds of good and ill,
> Through tempering of her words and lookes by wondrous skill.

Yet were her words and lookes but false and fayned,
    To some hid end to make more easie way,
    Or to allure such fondlings, whom she trayned
    Into her trap vnto their owne decay:
    Thereto, when needed, she could weepe and pray,
    And when her listed, she could fawne and flatter;
    Now smyling smoothly, like to sommers day,
    Now glooming sadly, so to cloke her matter;
Yet were her words but wynd, and all her teares but water.

                    (VI.vi.41–42)

They are mirrors not only of Crudor and Briana, but of each other as well, for Blandina will go out of her way to appear to please everyone, and Turpine has no sense whatsoever of appropriate behavior, deriding Calepine rather than coming to his aid with the wounded Serena and refusing the sanctuary of his home to those in need. In these actions Turpine is, of course, the precise opposite of both Calidore, who had come to Priscilla's aid unasked, and Aldus, who offered the courtesies of a good host in spite of his own problems.

The Salvage Man, who rescues Calepine and Serena from Turpine, is also Turpine's precise opposite and illustrates that courtesy is not restricted to those who reside in courts. He has neither weapons nor armor, he does not speak, and he eats only the fruits and vegetables he finds in nature (VI.iv.14). In short, Spenser is showing us in the Salvage Man the very essence of courtesy. The trappings of chivalry and chivalric behavior, wealth and the court, even language, are all ornaments of courtesy, but not its essence. Even those who lack all semblance of civilization are still capable of behaving courteously, while those who have those trappings—like Sir Turpine—may well lack the essential quality that should prompt them to courtesy. Already, then, less than half way through canto iv, Spenser has shown us that his etymological definition of courtesy at the opening of Book VI is insufficient. The word *courtesy* may well be derived from *court,* but courtesy in fact is as likely to be found elsewhere.

In showing us the opposing behaviors of Turpine and the Salvage

Man, Spenser also reveals a controversy regarding the source of human activity, which has continued into our own day: whether nature or nurture holds primacy in determining human behavior. Is courtesy a matter of breeding or of training? The first half of canto iv establishes the role of nature in courtesy. The second half seems to establish the role of nurture. The child whom Calepine rescues from a bear and gives to Matilda for her husband, the fortuitously named Sir Bruin, is in effect totally without nature, or at least we are not informed of his parentage. This lost or abandoned child is rescued from nature and turned over to Matilda and her husband to rear as they see fit. It would seem that Spenser is coming down unequivocally on the side of nurture, for the baby, he says, "became a famous knight well knowne / And did right noble dedes, the which elswhere are showne" (VI.iv.38). But he sees that the issue is never quite so clear, that we cannot be absolutely certain that nature has not also been at work. Uncertainty of parentage does not necessarily mean low birth:

> And certes it hath oftentimes bene seene,
>> That of the like, whose linage was vnknowne,
>> More braue and noble knights haue raysed beene,
>> As their victorious dedes haue often showne.
>> Being with fame through many Nations blowen,
>> Then those, which haue bene dandled in the lap.
>> Therefore some thought, that those braue imps were sowen
>> Here by the Gods, and fed with heauenly sap
> That made them grow so high t'all honorable hap.
>
> (VI.iv.36)

Canto iv does not provide us with a definitive answer in the nature/nurture debate, nor does it even make clear on which side Spenser stands. Rather, Spenser seems more intent on showing us how complex the terms of that debate are and that courtesy is where one finds it, unrestricted to any one social group and more important for itself than for its origins.

In the next canto we see a character who will prove to be still another mirror, this time for Calidore when he abandons his quest to live the pastoral life. The hermit with whom Prince Arthur leaves Timias and Serena for a cure proves to us that knights can retire—but also makes clear that there is a time for retirement, a point at which the knightly life is no longer appropriate. Calidore attempts to take early retirement in canto x and thus violates the code of behavior to which he is expected to adhere. This old knight, in retiring and becoming a hermit at an appropriate time, is able still to live an appropriate life and, in fact, to take advantage of his experience and wisdom, as he shows us in his sage advice to Timias and Serena about how to cure the wounds inflicted on them by the Blatant Beast.

Not until canto vi do we really get many details about the nature of the Blatant Beast, the object of Calidore's quest and the horrid monster who has injured both Serena and Timias. If there is a precise historical significance to the monster, it is not entirely clear; the Beast does, however, represent infamy or scandal, and the wounds it inflicts are incurable:

> No wound, which warlike hand of enemy
>   Inflicts with dint of sword, so sore doth light,
>   As doth the poysnous sting, which infamy
>   Infixeth in the name of noble wight:
>   For by no art, nor any leaches might
>   It euer can recured be againe;
>   Ne all the skill, which that immortal spright
>   Of *Podalyrius* did in it retaine
> Can remedy such hurts; such hurts are hellish paine.
>   (VI.vi.1)

The only remedy against its attack, as the hermit makes clear to Timias and Serena, is a self-cure. One must learn self-control and, more importantly, to "auoide the occasion of the ill . . . / Shun secresie, and talke in open sight" (VI.vi.14).

Leaving Timias behind with the Hermit to effect his cure, Arthur encounters not the Blatant Beast, but the two knights hired by Turpine to seek revenge on him. This episode brings us back once more, then, to questions of chivalric courtesy, for knights were forbidden by their commonly accepted code of behavior to sell their services. When Arthur slays one of the young knights, the other realizes his error and agrees to bring Turpine to Arthur. When they arrive, Turpine calls upon his former ally for aid, but the knight has clearly learned the importance of faith and good will to knightly behavior:

> Nathelesse for all his speach, the gentle knight
> Would not be tempted to such villenie,
> Regarding more his faith, which he did plight,
> All were it to his mortall enemie,
> Then to entrap him by false treachie.
>
> (VI.vii.23)

Arthur defeats Turpine and subjects him to a punishment fit for such a cowardly and discourteous knight, stripping him of his banner and hanging him upside down from a tree where all who pass can see his punishment "and by the like ensample warned bee" (VI.vii.27).

Having dispensed with Turpine, Spenser turns our attention in the second half of canto vii to Mirabella, one of the few overtly allegorical figures in this book, a "coy Damzell" (VI.vii.30) who has treated her suitors with disdain, for "none she worthie thought to be her fere, / But scornd them all, that loue vnto her ment" (VI.vii.29). Having been found guilty in Cupid's court for her treatment of his followers, she has been sentenced to a punishment that fits her crime: "Which was, that through this worlds wyde wildernes / She wander should in companie of those / Till she had sau'd so many loues, as she did lose" (VI.vii.37). While Mirabella is reminiscent of the Squire of Dames from Book III, she is a more sympathetic character, for her transgression is more psychological and social than purely sexual: she has not discarded her lovers as he did, but rather has rejected their suits, a violation not of sexual but of social mores. She is, in effect, the extreme of the Petrarchan mistress, the woman beloved of the poet who treats his advances with scorn and disdain, leading to the rejection and despair we find in conventional Petrarchan love poetry. Appropriately enough, she is accompanied by Scorne and Disdaine, the latter of whom attacks and defeats Timias at the end of the canto. Arthur defeats Disdaine in the next canto, but Mirabella intercedes, explaining her plight and making clear that she is indeed a disdainful woman on the model of the cruel Petrarchan love object:

> But let them loue that list, or liue or die;
> Me list not die for any louers doole:
> Ne list me leaue my loued libertie,
> To pitty him that list to play the foole:
> To loue my selfe I learned had in schoole.
> Thus I triumphed long in louers paine,
> And sitting carelesse on the scorners stoole,
> Did laugh at those that did lament and plaine.
> (VI.viii.21)

Her punishment, she realizes, is appropriate, and she must be allowed to continue her quest.

Having seen the extreme of the Petrarchan love object in Mirabella, we turn in the second half of canto viii to Serena and the "saluage nation," a group of primitive people who are a parody of Petrarchan admiration with their desire not to praise and love Mirabella, but rather to praise and eat her. The savages are as far from courteous as they are from civilization, practicing no useful arts and even resorting to cannibalism. But their responses to Serena are nonetheless reminiscent of the extremes of Petrarchan love poetry:

> Some with their eyes the daintest morsels chose;
> Some praise her paps, some praise her lips and nose;
> Some whet their kniues, and strip their elboes bare:
> The Priest him selfe a garland doth compose
> Of finest flowres, and with full busie care
> His bloudy vessels wash, and holy fire prepare.
> (VI.viii.39)

The difference between the savages and the Petrarchan lovers is, of course, the end they seek: the savages are interested in Serena not as a love object but as a meal, even though their desire degenerates to lust and must be controlled by the Priest. Appropriately enough, Serena is rescued from this feast by her lover Calepine.

Calepine and Serena reunited at last, we return in canto ix to Calidore, having last seen him six cantos earlier. But we turn our attention to him just in time to see him abandon his quest in favor of the pastoral life—or, more accurately, in favor of pursuing Pastorella, the object of his love. Such a life, he says, is far superior, for those who live it are

> Leading a life so free and fortunate,
> From all the tempests of these worldly seas,
> Which tosse the rest in daungerous disease;
> Where warres, and wreckes, and wicked enmitie
> Doe them afflict, which no man can appease.
> (VI.ix.19)

How wrong he is in this assessment he shall shortly learn. Unable to impress Pastorella with courtly behavior, Calidore abandons even his armor and weapons for shepherd's weeds and a staff. The following canto opens with explicit criticism of Calidore for abandoning his quest, but also an understanding of why he might wish to do so:

> Ne certes mote he greatly blamed be,
>> From so high step to stoupe vnto so low.
>> For who had tasted once (as oft did he)
>> The happy peace, which there doth ouerflow,
>> And rou'd the perfect pleasures, which doe grow
>> Amongst poore hyndes, in hils, in woods, in dales,
>> Would neuer more delight in painted show
>> Of such false blisse, as there is set for stales,
> T'entrap vnwary fooles in their eternall bales.
> (VI.x.3)

Furthermore, Spenser says, Calidore is in love and thus is even less to be blamed. After all, even the poet finds himself obliged to apologize to Gloriana for producing an interlude praising his own love:

> Sunne of the world, great glory of the sky
>> That all the earth does lighten with thy rayes,
>> Great *Gloriana,* greatest Maiesty,
>> Pardon thy shepheard, mongst so many layes,
>> As he hath sung of thee in all his dayes,
>> To make one minime of thy poore handmayd,
>> And vnderneath thy feete to place her prayse,
>> That when thy glory shall be farre displayd
> To future age of her this mention may be made.
>
> (VI.x.28)

Like Calidore, Spenser is momentarily distracted from his main task by his love.

The dance of the Graces on Mount Acidale is one of the most striking episodes in all of *The Faerie Queene,* for only here does Spenser show us himself, in the person of Colin, the poet-shepherd who was his spokesman in *The Shepheardes Calender.* The vision, in which the poet's love is surrounded by the three Graces who, in turn, are surrounded by "an hundred naked maidens, lilly white / All raunged in a ring, and dauncing in delight" (VI.x.11), vanishes instantly when Calidore moves into view. Calidore is even more out of place here than he is in the pastoral village; he is a warrior, not a poet. His quest is not Colin's, and the Graces vanish in his presence.[38] He may have tried to abandon his own world for pastoral pleasures, to attempt to become a lover, but as he will soon learn, when we try to abandon the cares of the world for a life of ease and grace, those very cares may seek us out. For following quickly on the heels of the mystical vision on Mount Acidale, the pastoral paradise is invaded and destroyed by the Brigands.

While courtesy is displayed even by the Brigand captain when he attempts to keep Pastorella from the slave traders, nonetheless the major lesson of this latter third of Book VI is that one cannot escape the duties of life—and perhaps that the pastoral ideal to which so many of Spenser's contemporaries subscribed is dead. The calm and beauty of the shepherd's life give way to murder and mayhem, and even the sheep fall under the reckless care of ignorant Brigands. Calidore may rescue Pastorella from the Brigands, even restore her to her true parents, but the life in which he found her, the world in which he found true peace and respite from his search for the Blatant Beast is destroyed in the process, and there is no returning to it. It is surely not coincidental that Spenser shows us himself in the person of Colin in this episode, for he must have realized from his vantage point in Ireland, facing the ever-encroaching Irish rebels, that the ideals of his pastoral life would also soon be lost, that return to the civilization of London life would be a matter more of necessity than of choice. Duty had brought him to Ireland as it brought Calidore to the pastoral village, and duty would call him home again, as it calls Calidore in the final half of canto xii back to his quest for the Blatant Beast.

And the Beast, though captured by Calidore, is loosed again upon the world at the end of this Book, and even there the poet personalizes the effects of this disastrous occurrence:

> Ne may this homely verse, of many meanest,
>> Hope to escape his venemous despite,
>> More than my former writs, all were they clearest
>> From blamefull blot, and free from all that wite,
>> With which some wicked tongues did it backebite,
>> And bring into a mighty Peres displesure,
>> That neuer so deserued to endite.
>> Therefore do you my rimes keep better measure,
> And seeke to please, that now is counted wisemens threasure.
>
> (VI.xii.41)

11

Conclusion:
"Eterne in Mutabilitie"

Book VI ends on what can only be called a depressing note, with the Blatant Beast loosed once more upon the world and even the poem itself subject to danger. Book VII, the "Cantos of Mutabilitie," provides a consolation for the apparent dejection of the sixth book.

We can never be absolutely certain of Spenser's intentions for the fragment called the "Cantos of Mutabilitie." This fragment is comprised of two complete cantos, marked vi and vii, and two additional stanzas at the opening of canto viii. It may well have been intended as the "allegorical center" of Book VII, although we have no clue about how that "center" would fit the remainder of the book. We do not, in fact, even know if there ever was a "remainder of the book." Did Spenser begin writing a new book with these cantos, then break off, for whatever reason? Did he have at hand the first five cantos as well? Did he intend the "Cantos of Mutabilitie" as a fit ending for a poem he knew he would never complete, or was his work cut short by the rebels who drove him out of Ireland or his death in 1599? Such questions, simply, cannot be answered.

Even the date of composition is uncertain. I've tried to suggest elsewhere that 1595 is the appropriate date, thus making the Cantos the last extant portion of *The Faerie Queene* to be composed, but others have suggested that they may have been written as early as 1580 or as late as 1598 and that, in fact, they may even have been a draft for an earlier portion of the poem or a completely separate entity.[39]

All we know for certain is that the Cantos first appear in an edition of *The Faerie Queene* published by Matthew Lownes in 1609 and that since that date they have appeared as the fragmentary Book VII. We can also see from the Cantos themselves that they reflect a concern with change found earlier in the poem, particularly in the proem to Book V, where Spenser laments the changes that have overtaken the world:

> For from the golden age, that first was named,
>   It's now at earst become a stonie one;
>   And men themselues, the which at first were framed
>   Of earthly mould, and form'd of flesh and bone,
>   Are now transformed into hardest stone.
>
> (V.p.2)

Briefly, these cantos concern themselves with the personified figure of Mutabilitie who, having proven her power on earth, attempts to overthrow the heavens as well:

> For, she the face of earthly things so changed,
>   That all which Nature had establisht first
>   In good estate, and in meet order ranged,
>   She did pervert, and all their statutes burst:
>   And all the worlds faire frame (which none yet durst
>   Of Gods or men to alter or misguide)
>   She alter'd quite, and made them all accurst
>   That God had blest; and did at first prouide
> In that still happy state for euer to abide.
> ....
> And now when all the earth she thus had brought
>   To her behest, and thralled to her might
>   She gan to cast in her ambitious thought,

Conclusion

> T'attempt the empire of the heauens hight,
> And *Ioue* himselfe to shoulder from his right.
>
> (VII.vi.5, 7)

Jove responds to her challenge by ordering that a trial be held on Arlo Hill, once a place favored by the gods but now quite changed.

In what initially appears to be a diversion, Spenser tells the story of Arlo Hill, a tale in the Ovidian manner, which explains how Ireland has gone from a place blessed by the gods to its present condition, a place cursed by Diana:

> To weet, that Wolues, where she was wont to space,
> Should harbour'd be, and all those Woods deface,
> And Thieues should rob and spoile that Coast around.
> Since which, those Woods, and all that goodly Chase,
> Doth to this day with Wolues and Thieues abound:
> Which too-too true that lands in-dwellers since haue found.
>
> (VII.vi.55)

This is not, in fact, a diversionary tale, but rather an example of the effects of mutability on earth, although Mutabilitie herself makes no appearance in the episode. The Ireland Spenser had known and loved in the 1580s and 1590s had been despoiled by rebels and thieves, fallen victim to time and change, and here he attempts to find some small consolation by making that change both mythological and purposeful.

In canto vii, Mutabilitie sets forth her case before Nature, the judge, bringing her parade of witnesses to prove that everything is subject to change: the four elements and all things made up of them, the seasons, the months, the hours, even Life and Death. This is, she thinks, sufficient to prove her powers:

> When these were past, thus gan the *Titanesse;*
> Lo, mighty mother, now be the iudge and say,
> Whether in all thy creatures more or lesse
> *CHANGE* doth not raign and beare the greatest sway:
> For, who sees not, that *Time* on all doth pray?

> But *Times* do change and moue continually.
> So nothing here long standeth in one stay:
> Wherefore, this lower world who can deny
> But to be subiect still to *Mutabilitie?*
>
> (VII.vii.47)

She even points to the planets, the manifestations of the gods themselves, as subject to her, changing constantly and wandering far from where we should expect to find them. Her case seems made, but Nature's response is swift and unequivocal:

> I well consider all that ye haue sayd,
>   And find that all things stedfastnes doe hate
>   And changed be: yet being rightly wayd
>   They are not changed from their first estate;
>   But by their change their being doe dilate:
>   And turning to themselues at length againe,
>   Doe worke their owne perfection so by fate:
>   Then ouer them Change doth not rule and raigne;
> But they raigne ouer change, and doe their states maintaine.
>
> (VII.vii.58)

Change is not the result of Mutabilitie's sway. It is, rather, the natural order, for that things will change is a constant upon which we can depend. And like the hours, the months, the seasons, change is cyclical, always returning to where it has been, constantly renewing, and in that renewal proving its immutability and immortality. And when such changes cease, it will not be a victory for Mutabilitie, for "from thenceforth, none no more change shall see" (VII.vii.59).

Mutabilitie, then, is caught in her own trap; she learns—as we should have learned—that the changes she ascribes to her own power are part of the natural order. Change is natural. Even if we do not recognize the immutability of cycles of change in the elements and the things of this earth, even in Life and Death, we certainly should see those cycles in the hours, the months, and the seasons, and we should recognize that they reflect our lives as well.

Conclusion

"The VIII. Canto, unperfite" is not just a fragment, two stanzas standing alone. Regardless of Spenser's intentions for these stanzas, as we have them they are the poet's parting remarks on mutability and on his poem. There will be change, mutability will seem to rule until "all shall rest eternally / With Him that is the God of Sabbaoth hight" (VII.viii.2). But until that time, the poem itself, the whole of *The Faerie Queene,* may demonstrate to us the proof of the principle of "eterne in mutability." The greatest promise of poetry is immortality: "So long as men can breathe, or eyes can see, / So long lives this, and this gives life to thee," Shakespeare says to the young man addressed in his sonnets (Sonnet 18). The same principle applies to *The Faerie Queene.* The centuries have passed. Spenser and his queen have long since left the earth. As living beings, they were subject to change. But in his poem they live on still to speak to us and teach us how better to become that ideal, the "gentleman or noble person" well trained "in vertuous and gentle discipline."

Notes and References

1. Letter to Ralegh. Here and throughout I quote from A. C. Hamilton's edition of *The Faerie Queene* (New York: Longman's, 1977); book, canto, and stanza numbers are indicated parenthetically following quotations from the poem.

2. See Gary Waller, *Mary Sidney, Countess of Pembroke* (Salzburg: Studies in English Literature, 1979), 53.

3. *The Defense of Poesy,* in *Sir Philip Sidney: Selected Prose and Poetry,* 2d ed., ed. Robert Kimbrough (Madison: University of Wisconsin Press, 1983), 108–9.

4. Samuel Johnson, "Preface to Shakespeare," in *The Great Critics,* 3d ed., ed. James Harry Smith and Edd Winfield Park (New York: Norton, 1951), 444.

5. Reprinted in *Edmund Spenser: The Critical Heritage,* ed. R. M. Cummings (New York: Barnes & Noble, 1971), 92; this compilation of early commentary on Spenser is an excellent source of such remarks, all gathered together in a single volume.

6. Dedication of Dryden's *Satires of Decimus Junious Juvenalis,* in Cummings's *Critical Heritage,* 202.

7. From Joseph Addison, *An Account of the Greatest English Poets,* in Cummings's *Critical Heritage,* 224.

8. *Lectures on the English Poets,* in *Edmund Spenser: A Critical Anthology,* ed. Paul Alpers (Baltimore: Penguin, 1969), 133–34. Readers looking for a more thorough examination of the critical reception should consult Alpers's book, not only for its selections from the major critical statements, but for its excellent introductory essays as well.

9. From Coleridge's notes in his copy of *The Faerie Queene,* in Alpers, *Edmund Spenser,* 146.

10. Lines 37–48, in *The Yale Edition of the Shorter Poems of Edmund*

Spenser, ed. William Oram et al. (New Haven: Yale University Press, 1989), 172–73.

11. C. S. Lewis, *English Literature in the Sixteenth Century* (Oxford: Oxford University Press, 1954), 363.

12. *The Defense of Poesy,* in Kimbrough, *Sir Philip Sidney,* 147.

13. In John R. Elliott's *The Prince of Poets* (New York: New York University Press, 1968), 4.

14. Preface to Greene's *Menaphon* (1589), in Elliott's *The Prince of Poets,* 6.

15. On this issue, see Thomas P. Roche, Jr., *The Kindly Flame: A Study of the Third and Fourth Books of Spenser's Faerie Queene* (Princeton: Princeton University Press, 1964), especially "The Nature of Allegory," 3–31.

16. This issue is examined in some detail by Kenneth Gross in "Mythology and Metrics in Spenser," *PMLA* 98 (1983); reprinted in Harold Bloom's *Edmund Spenser* (New York: Chelsea House, 1986), 211–18.

17. *The Princeton Encyclopedia of Poetry and Poetics,* enlarged ed., ed. Alex Preminger et al. (Princeton: Princeton University Press, 1974), 12.

18. Readers who would prefer a more comprehensive—and thus more accurate—definition of allegory in *The Faerie Queene* should consult Isabel MacCaffrey's *Spenser's Allegory: The Anatomy of Imagination* (Princeton: Princeton University Press, 1976).

19. Carolly Erickson, *The First Elizabeth* (New York: Summit Books, 1983), 324.

20. Ibid., 325.

21. This issue is examined by Jerome S. Dees in "The Narrator of *The Faerie Queene:* Patterns of Response," *TSLL* 12 (1970–71): 537–68.

22. *Troilus and Cressida,* Prologue, line 2.

23. *Spenser's Anatomy of Heroism* (Cambridge: Cambridge University Press, 1970), 116.

24. *Defense of Poesy,* in Kimbrough, *Sir Philip Sydney,* 128–29.

25. Many critics have observed that *The Faerie Queene* cannot be called "novelistic." See, for example, Thomas Roche's *The Kindly Flame* or Roger Sale's *Reading Spenser: An Introduction to The Faerie Queene* (New York: Random House, 1968).

26. Roche, *The Kindly Flame,* 76.

27. Both names appear: "Telamond" in the title, but "Triamond" in the text itself. Given the names of his brothers, Priamond and Diamond, "Triamond" seems the more likely choice.

28. Roche, *The Kindly Flame,* 200; interestingly, Roche's view would also

seem to imply that somehow the poem is then complete in its six books: the diptych can be closed.

29. Rosemary Freeman, *The Faerie Queene: A Companion for Readers* (Berkeley: University of California Press, 1970), 226.

30. Freeman, 227–28.

31. Roche, *The Kindly Flame,* 168.

32. For a more thorough examination of the concept of *discordia concors,* see Roche, *The Kindly Flame.*

33. This definition is from the *Oxford English Dictionary.* The issue of equity is covered by W. Nicholas Knight in "The Narrative Unity of Book V of *The Faerie Queene:* 'That Part of Justice Which is Equity,' " *RES,* n.s. 21 (1970): 267–94.

34. I Kings 25–26, quoted from the Geneva Bible.

35. In Hamilton's edition of *The Faerie Queene,* note to V.viii.28, quoting Camden's *History of Princess Elizabeth.*

36. In effect, Crudor and Briana are the physical embodiments of a verb: to *beard* someone is "to oppose openly and resolutely, with daring or with affrontery; to set at defiance, thwart, affront" (*Oxford English Dictionary*), a meaning that predates Spenser.

37. See A. Bartlett Giamatti, *Play of Double Senses: Spenser's Faerie Queene* (Englewood Cliffs, N.J.: Prentice-Hall, 1975), 98: "Book VI, the story of Calidore, mirror of Courtesy, is told through mirror scenes, each scene projecting a more elevated version of the ideal couple."

38. For examinations of the episode, see MacCaffrey, *Spenser's Allegory,* especially part 4, "Book VI: The Paradise Within," and Humphrey Tonkin, *Spenser's Courteous Pastoral: Book VI of The Faerie Queene* (Oxford: Clarendon, 1972).

39. In " 'Fixt in heauens hight': Spenser, Astronomy, and the Date of the *Cantos of Mutabilitie,*" *Spenser Studies* 4 (1984): 115–29, I have tried to demonstrate that the astronomical event portrayed by Spenser in the *Cantos* is a real lunar eclipse that occurred on 14 April 1595 and thus helps fix the date of Book VII. The first two paragraphs of that essay examine other views of the date and purpose of the *Cantos.*

Selected Bibliography

The following is an attempt to provide the reader with a basic, beginning bibliography of Spenser studies. It is hardly exhaustive; I have not even included all of the works referred to in the notes. The McNeir-Provost *Bibliography* contains some 2,600 entries for the period 1937–72; the bibliographic update in *Spenser Newsletter* lists an additional 1,400 or so entries up to 1986. Even considering that several of these entries are reprints, the study of Spenser is still obviously a growth industry and any attempt to be comprehensive in a short space can meet only with failure. Similarly, I have not tried to be up to date in these entries. The works I have listed would be considered by many rather dated, but most Spenserians would, I believe, regard them as essential, a good starting point for anyone seriously interested in pursuing study of *The Faerie Queene*. The *Spenser Encyclopedia* (University of Toronto Press, 1990) provides a great deal of information on virtually any subject, and for guides to the most recent work on Spenser, including not only books and articles but also conference papers, the interested reader should consult the pages of *Spenser Newsletter*.

Primary Works

Edmund Spenser: Books I and II of The Faerie Queene, The Mutability Cantos, and Selections from the Minor Poetry. Edited by Robert Kellogg and Oliver Steele. New York: Odyssey, 1965.

Selected Bibliography

Edmund Spenser: The Faerie Queene. Edited by A. C. Hamilton. New York: Longman's, 1977.

Edmund Spenser's Poetry. 2d ed., edited by Hugh Maclean. New York: W. W. Norton, 1982.

The Faerie Queene. Edited by Thomas P. Roche, Jr. New Haven: Yale University Press, 1981.

The Shepheardes Calender. A Facsimile Reproduction. Edited by S. K. Heninger, Jr. Gainesville, Fla.: Scholars' Facsimiles & Reprints, 1979.

The Works of Edmund Spenser. A Variorum Edition. 11 vols. Edited by Edwin Greenlaw et al. Baltimore: Johns Hopkins University Press, 1932–49.

The Yale Edition of the Shorter Poems of Edmund Spenser. Edited by William Oram et al. New Haven: Yale University Press, 1989.

Secondary Works

Bibliographies

Atkinson, Dorothy F. *Edmund Spenser: A Bibliographic Supplement.* Baltimore: Johns Hopkins University Press, 1937. Continues Carpenter's *Reference Guide* (listed below).

Carpenter, Frederic Ives. *A Reference Guide to Edmund Spenser.* New York: Kraus, 1969. A reprint of the bibliographic work covering early Spenser criticism first published in 1923.

McNeir, Waldo F., and Foster Provost. *Edmund Spenser: An Annotated Bibliography, 1937–1972.* Pittsburgh: Duquesne University Press, 1975. An expansion of the earlier edition of the bibliography, which covered the years 1937–60. Over 2,600 entries, arranged by work (and by book of *The Faerie Queene*), each with a brief annotation. Supplemented by the updates appearing in *Spenser Newsletter*.

Sipple, William, and Bernard Vondersmith. *Edmund Spenser: 1900–1936: A Reference Guide.* Boston: G. K. Hall, 1984. Excludes mere notices and other "marginal items" found in earlier bibliographies covering this period but "includes about 1,400 items directly related to Spenser studies" (p. vii).

Spenser Newsletter. Issued three times each year under the editorship of Darryl J. Gless, Department of English, University of North Carolina. The notices, abstracts, and reviews of recent articles and books make *Spenser Newsletter* the first place to look for the most recent work on Spenser. Since 1980 it has included the "Spenser Bibliography Update," compiled annually by John W. Moore, Jr., covering works published since 1972. The bibliography is not annotated, but it is arranged by work (and book of *The Faerie Queene*).

Collections of Essays

Alpers, Paul. *Edmund Spenser: A Critical Anthology*. Baltimore: Penguin, 1969. Selection of critical commentary from the earliest (E.K.'s "Dedicatory Epistle" to *The Shepheardes Calender*) to the late 1960s. The selections are valuable and so are Alpers's three introductory essays ("Contemporaneous Criticism," "Neoclassical and Romantic Criticism," and "Modern Views").

Bloom, Harold. *Edmund Spenser*. New York: Chelsea House, 1986. Part of Bloom's "Modern Critical Views" series; contains sixteen essays on Spenser, the earliest first published in 1963, the latest specifically written for the collection.

Cummings, R. M. *Edmund Spenser: The Critical Heritage*. New York: Barnes & Noble, 1971. A collection of appreciations, notices, and essays from the sixteenth through the early eighteenth centuries.

Elliott, John R., Jr. *The Prince of Poets: Essays on Edmund Spenser*. New York: New York University Press, 1968. Divided into five parts, "The Poet's Poet," "The Critic's Poet," "The Scholar's Poet," "The Minor Poems," and "*The Faerie Queene*," this collection provides a good overview of earlier criticism.

Hamilton, A. C. *Essential Articles: Edmund Spenser*. Hamden, Conn.: Archon Books, 1972. Thirty-one essays and selections from longer works on *The Faerie Queene* and five on the shorter poems.

Mclean, Hugh, ed. *Edmund Spenser's Poetry*. 2d ed. New York: Norton, 1982. A Norton Critical Edition, including selections from the poetry and a set of essays, mainly from the twentieth century.

Roche, Thomas P., Jr., and Patrick Cullen, eds. *Spenser Studies: A Renaissance Annual*. This hardbound annual publication issued by AMS Press contains essays mainly on Spenser but occasionally on other Renaissance poets as well. (Volume 1 is for 1981.)

Other Books

Alpers, Paul. *The Poetry of The Faerie Queene*. Columbia: University of Missouri Press, 1982. A reissue of Alpers's 1967 book (published originally by Princeton University Press). In his own words, Alpers says the book is "intended to bring *The Faerie Queene* into focus—to enable the ordinary reader and student to trust Spenser's verse, and scholars and critics to agree on what the realities of the poem are and on the ways in which it is profitable to discuss and investigate them" (p. vii). I doubt that anyone will ever create agreement on such issues, but Alpers's book continues to achieve its goals for the "ordinary reader and student."

Aptekar, Jane. *Icons of Justice: Iconography and Thematic Imagery in Book V of "The Faerie Queene."* New York: Columbia University Press, 1969. This book, in the author's words, is "based . . . in iconographical tradition [and] may suggest new attitudes, directions, and possibilities [as well as] help to explain a number of details in Spenser's text which have hitherto been under discussion, or obscure" (p. 5). A good corrective for those views of Book V that deal almost exclusively with the historical allegory.

Berger, Harry, Jr. *The Allegorical Temper: Vision and Reality in Book II of Spenser's "Faerie Queene."* New Haven: Yale University Press, 1957. Beginning with the problem of Guyon's swoon in canto vii, Berger examines Book II in terms of "Intellectual History" and "Allegorical Method" (to borrow from two of his section headings). This book is the place to start for a more thorough examination of Book II.

Cheney, Donald. *Spenser's Image of Nature: Wild Man and Shepherd in "The Faerie Queene."* New Haven: Yale University Press, 1966. Concerned with the "concept of Nature as the world external to the poet and the poet's art, as the sense of reality which the poem is trying to illuminate" (p. 1). See especially his third chapter, "Gardens of Adonis."

Dunseath, T. K. *Spenser's Allegory of Justice in Book V of "The Faerie Queene."* Princeton: Princeton University Press, 1968.

Fowler, Alastair. *Spenser and the Numbers of Time.* New York: Barnes & Noble, 1964. An understanding of this book and Fowler's numerological approach leads to a far better appreciation of the precision of Spenser's art. Fowler presents a wealth of information not just on *The Faerie Queene,* but also on Renaissance astrology and number symbolism.

Judson, Alexander C. *The Life of Edmund Spenser.* Baltimore: Johns Hopkins University Press, 1945. Volume 11 of the *Variorum* edition; of necessity often very speculative, but nonetheless useful.

Lewis, C. S. *The Allegory of Love: A Study in Medieval Tradition.* 1936. Reprint. New York: Oxford University Press, 1968. See especially chapter 7, "*The Faerie Queene.*"

———. *English Literature in the Sixteenth Century.* Oxford: Clarendon, 1954. An extensive survey of English Renaissance literature; dated but still provocative.

MacCaffrey, Isabel G. *Spenser's Allegory: The Anatomy of Imagination.* Princeton: Princeton University Press, 1976. To better understand the allegory of Spenser's poem (or any other, for that matter), begin with this book.

Nohrnberg, James. *The Analogy of The Faerie Queene.* Princeton: Princeton University Press, 1976. At over 800 pages, this book "attempts to offer a critically unified commentary on *The Faerie Queene*" (p. ix)—and nearly succeeds.

Roche, Thomas P., Jr. *The Kindly Flame: A Study of the Third and Fourth Books of Spenser's "Faerie Queene."* Princeton: Princeton University Press, 1964. Still the book to read for an overview and interpretation of Books III and IV.

Tonkin, Humphrey. *Spenser's Courteous Pastoral: Book VI of "The Faerie Queene."* Oxford: Clarendon, 1972. Certainly the best study of Book VI.

Tuve, Rosamund. *Allegorical Imagery.* Princeton: Princeton University Press, 1966. A must for any student of Renaissance literature, especially of *The Faerie Queene.*

Waller, Gary. *English Poetry of the Sixteenth Century.* New York: Longman's, 1986. Only chapter 6 is specifically devoted to *The Faerie Queene,* but students of Spenser will find the entire book a good introduction to the experience of reading sixteenth-century poetry.

Williams, Kathleen. *Spenser's World of Glass: A Reading of "The Faerie Queene."* Berkeley: University of California Press, 1966. A reading of the entire poem, with particular attention to "the structural themes which work through several of the books, and the expanding net of images, all interlocking to form the microcosm of the poem" (p. xvii).

Index

Index

Index

The Author

Russell J. Meyer received his Ph.D. from the University of Minnesota in 1976. He has taught, mainly Spenser and Shakespeare, at the University of Missouri-Columbia and is currently professor and chair of the English Department at the University of Houston–Downtown.